VICTOR DE LA FUENTE

# THE INCONVENIENT TRUTH ABOUT BITCOIN

# THE INCONVENIENT TRUTH ABOUT BITCOIN

BTC book as utopian promise from financial system to get-rich-quick ponzi scheme

- Víctor de la Fuente -

Copyright © 2025 The inconvenient truth about Bitcoin

All rights reserved. No part of this publication may be reproduced, distributed, or transmitted in any form or by any means, including photocopying, recording, or other electronic or mechanical methods, without the prior written permission of the publisher, except in the case of brief quotations embodied in critical reviews and certain other noncommercial uses permitted by copyright law.

The inconvenient truth about Bitcoin / Víctor de la Fuente – 1st Edition

ISBN 9798321001455

# INDEX

Disclaimer

The inconvenient truth about Bitcoin and the only section you should read

Latest developments, same dangers

It is not Bitcoin all that glitters

Attacking Bitcoin is not defending an old-school system

**THE REAL PROBLEM**

- Slowness as Achilles heel: a 10-minute wait
- That roller coaster called Bitcoin and the insecurity of volatility
- The Myth of Decentralization
- What will happen if there are no miners to keep the gold?
- Under the shadow of a ponzi scheme
- Use cases and actual use cases are two totally different things
- El Salvador, An Oasis without Bitcoin
- Alt-coins: alternatives to nothing
- YouTube, trolls, and other nonsense

**A FINAL WORD**

- 'Finfluencers' and toxicity
- Conclusions

Resources

About Víctor de la Fuente

Other books by the author

## DISCLAIMER

I start the book in an unusual way because of the transparent and direct. Transparency is what we should demand from all those influencers, advisors, and, ultimately, those people who, at the very least, have opinions on a subject or, for the most part, try to influence it in one way or another for reasons hidden from their audience. More clearly, it does not invalidate an influencer's opinion or financial advice by holding Bitcoins, but, as we will see later, maybe it does have a bias and a hidden interest for the audience - promoting their use - simply because it suits them.

For the sake of that transparency, I bought Bitcoin through Kraken when BTC was worth around 320 USD. At the time, I bought 3 BTCs. Before you read on and get the wrong idea: I am not a crypto-millionaire - or a millionaire in any way.

If I got into BTC it is because I have a tech profile and certain financial notions. I liked his utopian proposal and had a low ticket. But if I told you before that I am not a crypto millionaire, it is that, at that time, you can also imagine how volatile it was and, above all, how niche BTC was. So within a few months, I sold all three of those BTCs.

Later, in one of the BTC turmoils, back in late 2020, I had everything set up so I could jump on that wave. At that time, I made a substantial amount of money buying and selling within a few weeks. True, I did not win everything I could have gained, neither at that time nor in view of the evolution to date. At the same time, I also did not lose money as I would have at the time of the sale.

It is easy in hindsight to know what the right moves are. Believe me if I write without the rancor or missed opportunity; on the contrary, I write from the experience and gratitude of having learned over all these years about the crypto world.

More importantly, if I sold at first, it was because I did not want to keep an eye on such a volatile asset, and because, despite the idealism behind it, I saw serious difficulties in its adoption - which I will detail at length in the book. If I bought back to sell in 2020, it was simply speculation.

And even more importantly, if I have not bought back and do not plan to buy BTC in the near or distant future, it is precisely because I *do not believe* in BTC. In part, it has lost not only the ideal, but also its structural problems.

The book is not an entry into a personal finance course. The book is not a gateway for you to buy any other cryptocurrency in which you do have investments instead of Bitcoin - spoiler: I have no investments in cryptocurrencies, Bitcoin, or any. The book is not an argument that BTC is a waste of money - I myself have won with BTC.

The book only tries to shed light on an asset -BTC- in which the discourse around it is not only manipulated by some interests but over-compensated in the arguments in favor against it.

# THE INCONVENIENT TRUTH ABOUT BITCOIN AND THE ONLY SECTION YOU SHOULD READ

It is curious that although surely with a single argument would be enough to knock all the smoke behind Bitcoin, its own definition and different use and misrepresentation of Bitcoin causes to have to add as many arguments as possible. By themselves they would be powerful enough to question Bitcoin.

The problem is twofold: just because its definition differs according to the person concerned, the conversation turns to one type of argument or another, many of them circular and contradictory. For starters, a symptom of this is that cryptocurrencies increasingly lose their last name and remain in the term 'cryptos.' Beyond a linguistic question, it is a way to hide something obvious: no cryptocurrency is used as currency; except to buy other currencies.

The second paradox is that, although one argument would be enough, being forced to add as many arguments as possible, it only dilutes the potency of that argument and opens up many other avenues of discussion that, although minor, end up dominating the conversation and never resolving the big issues. Big issues, so obvious, that to know them is impossible to think that they are incorrect because otherwise it would mean that *everyone* is wrong.

A Bitcoin transaction, a simpler language purchase, takes an average of about 10 minutes in its simplest form of validation. Bitcoin's scalability problem as a currency is unquestionable due to its extreme slowness (1) when each purchase takes 10 minutes and it is not a problem that is solved by adding more computing. Imagine being in a coffee shop, paying for tea and waiting 10 minutes until the transaction is completed so that they serve it to you. Now imagine there are three people in front of you and you have to wait half an hour. It does not make any sense.

Just as it makes no sense, due to the paradox of austerity, that as a financial asset will always rise; proposition of many crypto gurus. As a financial asset, it does not give you recurring dividends and if it always rises you will only want to sell it at the time of liquidating your investment. In this scenario, Bitcoin always rises in the long run, you will never want to use it as currency because if you had waited a little longer (minutes, hours, or days) you could buy more things. (2)

Moreover, its current volatility also prevents the consumer and the business from adopting it as currency (3). If you buy something with a value of 0.1 BTC and after 10 minutes or 10 days, the value of BTC has changed significantly, maybe you are more interested in returning that product to have your revalued 0.1 BTC and exchange them to USD or EUR. It is true that volatility is a dimension that can change and is not intrinsic to the design of the Bitcoin structure but, so far, volatility is a property exploited by many to make money in Day trading and speculation.

As if that were not enough, due to that volatile property that makes it an extremely attractive asset for speculators causes them to become guarantors of the asset for the interests they have in it and, therefore, become a pyramid system (4).

In the meantime, it is a question of the dialog being based on other concepts and not on the structural problems mentioned or others such as global viability in both environmental and economic fields. Due to its intensive energy and water consumption, in addition to the very structure and incentives towards Bitcoin miners and process such as halving, it is likely that in the near future it will not be profitable to mine Bitcoins or maintain the network (5).

The dialog is diverted to theoretical concepts and use cases instead of real use (6) since, today, the use of Bitcoin or cryptocurrencies, as currencies, is not limited but nonexistent.

Theoretical concepts such as the decentralization of the currency is at least questionable since, currently, there is a high concentration of both Bitcoin holders and miners (7).

Given all of this, it is only utopian that Bitcoin becomes the solution to the current monetary system. Among other reasons, in addition to those set out above, it is simply because it is an empty currency and without any form of backing (8). That is, Bitcoin and cryptocurrencies are monetary systems without support, means that they are based on nothing 'real' (meaning real by tangible).

If you buy shares, you literally have a share of the company. If you buy gold, you have a block of a material. If you buy a house, you have a place to sleep (or rent). If you buy Bitcoin, the "only" thing you have is Bitcoin. You cannot trade it for anything or have any legal rights to Bitcoin. All you have is a digital token saying that you have that token with no association to any 'real' asset and you have no legal right to anything. I insist, you only have one token. It is true that it is not so problematic because, if an asset is purely digital, it does not detract from its value per se. The same could be said of swords in World of Warcraft and the entire digital assets market for gaming and avatars.

If we live in a world where there is some consensus that such a token is worth a considerable amount, it is partly because of an illusion and perception created on the basis of different interests, in which millions of people and companies participate, but do not make it more or less valid and remains a very high-risk investment.

Add to that a Bitcoin property that is usually presented as a benefit: its scarcity. This shortage of up to 21 million BTC coins to be mined would create some stability. The fact is that, while flawed, we have already had a monetary system based on a limited asset (gold). The problem is that when there are huge demands for money, if you are not able to literally print more money like in the current monetary system, you can get people with debt to go bankrupt or there's massive deflation. Precisely the crisis of 2008 or the Covid period, even though the situation was dramatic, was not so much because governments could print more money. If these specific facts - or perhaps thinking that the market should be self-regulating - do not justify a system based on scarcity versus the many other ills that a system like the current one may have, it is something that escapes slightly from the objective of the book because it would open the discussion too much.

The book is not a defense of all the problems that the current financial system has. To be clear: that cash is currently being devalued does not mean that, however much consensus (or smoke) is behind it, the solution is Bitcoin for all the reasons described.

The uncomfortable truth is that, of everything written about BTC, the only prediction about Bitcoin that will come true from all that you've read is that... the year will end and you won't have bought anything with BTC (except other cryptocurrencies). Despite the enthusiasm, the news proclaiming its massive adoption, the influencers promoting it on social media, and the apocalyptic or utopian predictions about its future, the reality is more mundane. Stores that accept Bitcoin are still few and far between. Those who boast about their Bitcoin gains, more often than not, simply hold onto it in the hope that its value will skyrocket.

At the end of the day, the actual use of Bitcoin for everyday transactions remains more of a promise than a practice. It's not that Bitcoin lacks potential; it's that this potential has yet to be realized in the daily lives of most people. You might end the year having learned a lot about cryptocurrencies, having read about their technological advances, and perhaps even having invested in them. But when it comes to buying a pizza, paying the rent, or purchasing anything other than other cryptocurrencies, your Bitcoin wallet will remain untouched.

For many, Bitcoin is still a speculative asset rather than a functional currency. Fluctuations in its value, concerns about security, and the lack of widespread adoption by mainstream businesses mean that, for now, its primary use is as an investment. So yes, of all the predictions you may have read, the one that is sure to come true is that you will reach the end of the year and you won't have bought anything with Bitcoin other than other cryptocurrencies.

Víctor de la Fuente

# LATEST DEVELOPMENTS, SAME DANGERS

The landscape of cryptocurrency regulation has seen significant developments in 2025, largely centered around a period dubbed "Crypto Week" where lawmakers aimed to establish a comprehensive framework for digital assets in the United States. While three pieces of legislation were on the docket, only one, the Genius Act, successfully passed both the House and the Senate, marking a pivotal moment as the first major national cryptocurrency legislation in the US. This act, standing for "guiding and establishing national innovation for US stable coins," specifically focuses on providing a legal framework for payment stablecoins, which are cryptocurrencies designed to peg their value to a fiat currency, most commonly the US dollar, offering a more stable alternative to volatile assets like Bitcoin for transactions.

The Genius Act introduces a new registration regime for US dollar stablecoin issuers, mandating that only permitted payment stablecoin issuers (PPSIs) can issue these digital assets. These PPSIs are now required to back their stablecoins at least one-to-one with US coins, currency deposits, or short-term money market loans and securities, such as Treasury bonds and bills with maturities under 93 days. Transparency is a cornerstone of the new law, compelling issuers to publicly disclose their redemption policies, establish timely redemption procedures, and publish the monthly composition of their reserves, with these disclosures needing monthly certification by a registered public accounting firm. Furthermore, the act significantly enhances consumer protections by requiring issuers to segregate reserve assets from their own, imposing strict limitations on how these reserves can be used or invested, and prohibiting them from being pledged as collateral for any purpose other than creating liquidity for redemptions. Crucially, in the event of an issuer's bankruptcy, the Genius Act grants token holders priority over creditors in the distribution of reserve assets, a meaningful update for the crypto space where previously, investor funds were often considered lost in such scenarios. Stablecoin issuers are also now subject to the Bank Secrecy Act, meaning they must build client profiles, keep records, and flag large or suspicious transactions to combat anti-money laundering, aligning them with traditional financial institutions. Oversight for federally registered stablecoins will primarily fall under the Office of the Comptroller of the Currency (OCC), which oversees US banks, while smaller issuers (under $10 billion market cap) can opt for state-level regulation if comparable frameworks exist. However, the act explicitly states that stablecoins will not be defined as securities or commodities, thus exempting them from the jurisdiction of the Securities Exchange Commission (SEC) or the Commodity Futures Trading Commission (CFTC), suggesting a potentially less stringent oversight compared to traditional financial assets. While specific capital, liquidity, and risk management requirements are yet to be determined by regulators, the law also instructs the Secretary of the Treasury to investigate indigenously collateralized stablecoins, indicating a forward-looking approach to future regulation. The Genius Act is set to come into effect either 18 months after enactment or 120 days after primary federal regulators issue final implementing regulations, whichever comes first, though a grace period for non-permitted issuers extends until July 18, 2028, or three years post-enactment.

The Genius Act has been met with both celebration and criticism. Advocates laud it as a crucial step towards mainstream adoption of cryptocurrency, offering guardrails to prevent abuse in the space. Some believe it could bolster the US dollar's global dominance, given that 99% of stablecoins are already dollar-pegged and popular in emerging markets like India, Nigeria, and Indonesia, potentially increasing the usage of US dollar-based assets and even boosting the Treasury bond market by creating demand for US debt. The regulation is also considered more competitive than Europe's MiCA regulations, which require significant stablecoin issuers to hold 60% of reserves as deposits with traditional institutions, making the US a more attractive base for issuers. The establishment of a legal framework is expected to encourage industry incumbents like banks and PayPal to enter the stablecoin space. Conversely, critics argue the law doesn't go far enough to protect consumers, viewing it as a form of deregulation. Concerns include the law granting tech companies access to financial services with less traditional regulatory oversight, the absence of third-party audit requirements (distinct from internal accountant certification), and the lack of a federal insurance program akin to bank deposits, leaving users vulnerable to losses from issuer mismanagement. The legislation's language is also considered vague, with terms like "timely redemption" lacking specific definitions. The act's implications for foreign issuers, such as Tether, based in El Salvador with reserves that currently wouldn't meet the new requirements, raise questions about whether the US will cut off such stablecoins or accept less stringent "substantially similar" regulations, potentially introducing more risk to US users. Furthermore, some lament that the "know your client" (KYC) requirements detract from a core appeal of cryptocurrency – its removal from traditional regulations and controls. The act's passage, amidst significant lobbying by cryptocurrency companies and a president with personal interests in crypto's proliferation, also drew criticism.

Beyond the Genius Act, two other proposed pieces of legislation, though not yet passed by the Senate, illuminate the ongoing debates surrounding crypto regulation. The Anti-CBDC Surveillance State Act aims to preserve the private nature of stablecoins and prohibit the Federal Reserve from issuing its own central bank digital currency (CBDC), driven by concerns that a CBDC would grant the central bank excessive power, oversight, and control over individual finances. This act explicitly bans the Federal Reserve from issuing or using CBDCs for monetary policy and from offering financial products or services directly to individuals. While seen as more partisan and touching on "conspiracies" about Federal Reserve control, it reflects a strong sentiment against government-controlled digital currencies, despite the Federal Reserve not having confirmed plans for a CBDC.

The second significant proposed bill, the Clarity Act (formerly the Digital Asset Market Clarity Act), seeks to establish a comprehensive regulatory framework for all cryptocurrencies other than stablecoins, aiming to clarify jurisdictional boundaries within the crypto industry. This act proposes defining different categories: "digital commodities," such as Bitcoin and Ethereum, which are sufficiently decentralized and do not confer rights to profits, governance, or financial claims against an issuer, and "restricted digital assets," which encompass everything else that does. Under this framework, digital commodities would be exempt from securities laws and regulated by the Commodity Futures Trading Commission (CFTC), leading to much less stringent regulations and disclosure requirements for their issuers. Restricted digital assets, however, would fall under SEC governance. The Clarity Act also introduces anti-money laundering (AML) and KYC requirements for certain digital commodity-based companies and establishes a new registration category for companies in the space, a long-standing request from cryptocurrency exchanges that previously faced lawsuits for improper registration.

The Clarity Act, like its passed counterpart, faces considerable criticism. It's noted that it could benefit Donald Trump's own cryptocurrencies by helping them avoid SEC registration and oversight. More broadly, critics argue that for "meme coins," the act effectively signals "game on," as it seemingly demonstrates no intent to crack down on this sector. Despite the SEC having clarified that such tokens wouldn't be subject to their oversight, the Clarity Act provides virtually no regulatory oversight and minimal disclosure requirements for projects often associated with stealing investor money through fee skimming or "rug pulls". This leads some to label the Clarity Act as a form of deregulation in the investment space, potentially benefiting the price of certain cryptocurrencies but retaining significant risk within the system.

These legislative efforts emerge in a dynamic market, where Bitcoin itself reached new all-time highs in 2025, contributing to a $4 trillion valuation for the entire cryptocurrency sector. Earlier in 2024, a significant rally in Bitcoin's price, from around $26,000 to $49,000, was heavily influenced by the approval of Bitcoin spot Exchange Traded Funds (ETFs). The SEC had previously resisted such approvals due to concerns about market manipulation, but a legal victory by Grayscale ultimately led to the approval of 11 spot Bitcoin ETFs, making Bitcoin exposure more accessible through regulated financial institutions. However, Bitcoin's price actually fell after the ETF launch, possibly due to a "buy the rumor, sell the news" phenomenon and lower-than-expected net inflows compared to forecasts, alongside significant outflows from high-fee funds like Grayscale and sales by entities like the FTX estate. Even with these new investment vehicles, the SEC chair, Gary Gensler, publicly warned that Bitcoin remains a "speculative volatile asset" used for "illicit activity," and many traditional Wall Street firms continue to abstain from offering Bitcoin products, suggesting continued caution from mainstream finance.

Adding another layer to the regulatory conversation is the rise of "Bitcoin Treasuries," companies that hold Bitcoin on their balance sheets, a strategy popularized by MicroStrategy. This trend, often dubbed an "infinite money glitch," has seen some of these companies trade at a significant premium to the value of the Bitcoin they hold, attracting investors seeking exposure to the cryptocurrency through a publicly traded entity. While proponents highlight the strategic leverage and financing options these companies employ, critics view it as a gimmick capitalizing on investor enthusiasm, especially as some of these companies have questionable financials and their stock prices surge simply upon announcing Bitcoin acquisitions, a phenomenon reminiscent of the dot-com bubble. The broader cryptocurrency space continues to grapple with fundamental issues such as inherent high risk, speculative nature, lack of intrinsic value, and extreme volatility, making it an unstable basis for a currency or a reliable long-term investment, concerns that persist even as regulatory frameworks begin to emerge. These regulatory efforts, while providing some guardrails, are still far from transforming crypto's "wild west" reputation, leaving many questions about their ultimate impact on broader adoption and market stability.

The absence of an intrinsic value model for Bitcoin, as many financial professionals would define it, forces one to acknowledge that its price appreciation is often detached from fundamental demand, tied instead to the speculative impulses of those seeking quick gains.

This leads us to the undeniable speculative nature of crypto investments, a realm where one engages not in traditional investing, but in speculation. The market is frequently characterized by "inflated demand" where individuals purchase assets solely in anticipation of future price increases.

This environment fosters a "fanaticism" where an uncritical belief in ever-increasing prices fuels further demand, often from individuals with limited financial education who are convinced of Bitcoin's inevitability as the currency or safe haven of the future. Such fervent conviction, coupled with the absence of a "tried and true method for determining its value," underscores the extreme risk inherent in expecting continuous double-digit returns from non-producing assets. The notion of an "infinite money glitch," often associated with Bitcoin Treasuries, exemplifies this speculative excess, where companies with "questionable financials" see their stock prices surge simply by announcing Bitcoin acquisitions, mirroring the dot-com era's irrational exuberance.

Beyond these systemic issues, the realm of Decentralized Finance (DeFi), despite its promise of peer-to-peer transactions outside institutional influence, presents its own set of technical and operational dangers. DeFi systems are often "inefficient and cumbersome," consuming vast amounts of power; a single Ethereum transaction, for example, can consume significantly more electricity than tens of thousands of credit card transactions. Users face "high gas fees" for even basic functions, and more complex operations incur even greater costs. A critical impediment to widespread adoption is the problem of "over collateralization" for loans, where borrowers must deposit more money than they take out due to the inability to assess risk in an anonymous system. This vastly reduces the practical use cases for DeFi loans compared to traditional financial systems. Crucially, in DeFi, "consumer protections are... non-existent"; if one's cryptocurrencies are lost due to a scam, hack, or forgotten password, there is "absolutely no recourse for getting your coins back". While the blockchain itself boasts resilience, vulnerabilities often arise in the "human-coded smart contracts" that power DeFi applications. These bugs, once exploited by hackers, are difficult to patch due to the immutable nature of the blockchain, often requiring entire systems to be replaced, leading to slow and tedious remediation. Alarmingly, DeFi has, in many instances, begun to "replicate many of the problems of the system that it's looking to replace," including the development of derivatives like Collateralized Debt Obligations (CDOs), instruments central to the 2008 financial crisis.

Bitcoin can be worth 150.000 USD or 0 USD; and still, you never bough something with Bitcoin -and you don't know anyone that bought anything with any crypto-.

# IT IS NOT BITCOIN ALL THAT GLITTERS

The impetus behind writing this book stems from a concern about the lack of widespread financial culture and the need to bring perspective to an issue surrounded by sensationalism and often driven by questionable interests, to say the least. The emergence, demise, and subsequent resurgence of Bitcoin and other cryptocurrencies has captured the imagination of the public and investors - literally their imagination because there is no real or tangible use other than speculation - generating a whirlwind of media attention and speculation that often overshadows a more productive and critical debate about these assets and their place in the broader financial landscape.

In a world where news and analysis are often over-hyped and frantically searched for clicks - thanks to clickbaiting - it is easy to get lost in sensational narratives that speak of fortunes made overnight and technological revolutions that promise to radically transform society. Behind this façade of enthusiasm and optimism, however, is a complex reality waiting to be analyzed. The story of Bitcoin and cryptocurrencies in general is as much a tale of innovation and disruptive potential as a warning about the risks of speculation, volatility, and manipulation by well-resourced players.

The sensationalism around Bitcoin and other cryptocurrencies often stems from an amalgam of intertwined interests, including investment firms, trading platforms, social media influencers, and other actors who benefit directly from increased investment and attention in this sector. Such hype can distort public perception and lead to ill-informed investment decisions, especially among those who are new to the financial arena and may not be fully aware of the risks involved.

The lack of a strong financial culture leaves the general public vulnerable to this kind of sensationalism. In addition, due to the widespread crisis, the loss of purchasing power, and many other factors, this group is especially vulnerable and open to all kinds of avenues that promise shortcuts to get rich, effortlessly, without risk and without understanding the system itself. Without such a clear understanding of basic financial principles, economic history, and the nature of investments and speculative assets, it is difficult for individuals to discern between legitimate opportunities and risky or outright fraudulent schemes. This book aims to be an antidote to this trend, providing a balanced and evidence-based analysis that can serve as a guide to understanding Bitcoin and the cryptocurrency phenomenon.

By addressing financial culture and education as core issues, this book not only seeks to demystify Bitcoin and cryptocurrencies, but also to foster greater financial understanding that can empower individuals to make more informed and prudent decisions as a very secondary goal. The intention is to go beyond the surface of sensationalism and clickbaiting to explore the underlying realities of cryptocurrencies and, in particular, Bitcoin, their functioning, their potential impacts on the global economy and the risks they entail. With this approach, the book aims to provide readers with the tools needed to navigate the complex world of cryptocurrencies with a more critical and knowledge-based perspective.

The ultimate catalyst for writing this book was the response to a short video I posted on YouTube about Bitcoin, whose public reactions were as fascinating as they were revealing, highlighting a mix of illogical enthusiasm, lack of understanding of basic concepts, and a series of widespread misunderstandings about what Bitcoin really stands for, as well as various insults. The range of responses, from wholehearted support to uninformed criticism, highlighted the need for a more grounded approach to discussing this issue than a YouTube comment and response or a 7-minute video on the topic could provide. I was so struck by the comments and response to the video that I felt an immediate obligation to address the prevailing narrative, leading to the creation of a book that aspires to be direct and easy to understand.

The video basically focused on the fact that the value of Bitcoin, until now, is more due to the movement of people than its actual use. The reactions reflected the wide range of perceptions and the level of polarization around the cryptocurrency. Many users showed blind faith in Bitcoin as a financial panacea, ignoring its problems and limitations. At least, they kept a critical perspective on BTC.

This spectrum of responses exposed a significant gap in understanding of an asset that may indeed be difficult for many to comprehend, in addition to, I stress, a division between perception and reality, fueled by biased information, speculation, and often a lack of financial and technological context. Observing this gap led me to conclude that it was crucial to develop a straightforward essay that not only provided information and analysis about Bitcoin, but also challenged readers to think critically about the information they consume and the beliefs around it.

Writing a book that was straightforward and easy to understand became an essential goal in ensuring that the message was accessible to a wide audience, including those who, without prior experience in finance or technology, could understand. At the same time, that vision of getting straight to the point is even more incisive for all those self-proclaimed cryptocurrency gurus for being more difficult to rebut or to evade discussion. The intention is to cut through the noise and confusion, introducing Bitcoin in a way that is easy to digest, but without sacrificing rigor. This approach seeks to empower readers with the knowledge necessary to critically evaluate Bitcoin, understanding both its promises and its limitations.

The urgency of addressing the simplistic and often extreme narratives surrounding Bitcoin is crucial as biased discourse is established that can have a real impact on less informed collectives. In short, the response to the video in this book serves as a turning point, a call to action to contribute to a more informed and balanced conversation about Bitcoin in society. A shame about all the toxicity around.

My ideology, not only with Bitcoin but generally with technology, is not to adopt a ludicrous or anti-technological stance, but rather to balance the current debate that often seems one-sided, leaning heavily toward the uncritical adoption of technologies like Bitcoin, without an analysis of their implications. The central concern is that the prevailing discourse around cryptocurrencies, and especially Bitcoin, rarely undergoes scrutiny, leading to the acceptance of ideas and narratives without questioning their fundamentals or fully understanding their consequences. The same goes for other kinds of technologies, like the metaverse, which are also quite prone to inflamed sensationalism without the same critical thinking that they deserve.

In an environment where technology is advancing rapidly, there is a tendency to idealize these technological innovations, attributing to them the power to solve complex problems without recognizing the new challenges they may introduce. Paradoxically, moreover, the problems these technologies are trying to solve are usually problems generated by the same technology. This vision, often driven by technological enthusiasm and optimism, can overlook critical aspects such as ethical, social, economic, and environmental considerations.

This essay seeks to foster critical thinking, not only in the Bitcoin context but also in the broader scope of techno-philosophy, studying the relationship between technology and philosophical questions about life, society, and ethics. By focusing on Bitcoin, the book uses this cryptocurrency as a paradigm of study to explore how technology can influence the global economy, social systems, and individual values, and how our understanding and approach to it can reflect and shape our view of the technological world.

The goal is to demystify the notion that emerging technologies are inherently good or bad, and instead present a nuanced analysis that considers both their potential benefits and their potential risks and costs. The point is to recognize that while technology has the power to transform society in positive ways, its implementation and development must be carefully guided by its long-term impact and the fairness of its distribution and use.

The hope that Bitcoin could be the answer to several problems in the classic financial world is understandable, given its innovative nature and the disruptive promises that accompany it. Many, including me, have wanted to see Bitcoin as a definitive solution to issues like financial exclusion, runaway inflation, corruption, and reliance on over-empowered financial intermediaries. However, upon closer examination, it becomes clear that

Bitcoin not only fails to solve many of these problems, but also introduces new dilemmas and complications.

I fully understand the appeal of the Bitcoin promise. It is presented as a challenge to the established financial system, characterized by inequality and an environment in which the rich are becoming richer. In this context, Bitcoin has been projected as an escape route, an empowerment tool that offers the possibility of a more equitable system, where each individual can have control over their financial assets without the intermediation of banks or traditional institutions. This view has strong appeal, especially to those who feel marginalized or disadvantaged by the current system, offering a glimmer of hope that change is possible and that technology can be a catalyst for economic justice.

Many have taken advantage of Bitcoin's appeal to orchestrate schemes and frauds that promise big returns and quick riches. In some cases, these tactics have been targeted specifically at people with little financial knowledge or desperate to find a solution to their economic precariousness. Bitcoin's volatility, coupled with the lack of regulation in many territories, has created an ideal environment for malicious actors seeking to exploit people's hope and despair.

One of my focal points of the book is that this behavior does not correspond to 'a few' but in general to the fact that the Bitcoin system, with all its advantages, is cursed from its design and, therefore, is an empty promise.

My intention in writing this book is not to subvert the conviction of those who firmly believe in Bitcoin, many of whom invest in this cryptocurrency with unwavering faith in its potential to transform the financial world. However, I harbor some hope, perhaps naive, in planting a seed of doubt or curiosity that will encourage people to question and critically analyze the prevailing discourse about Bitcoin, a discourse that, at times, seems increasingly removed from the tangible and complex reality that characterizes this cryptocurrency.

Bitcoin, with its narrative of decentralization, resistance to censorship, and potential for financial autonomy, has captured - and captured - the imagination of millions. In a world awash in information and often dominated by extremely optimistic or pessimistic voices about Bitcoin, it becomes crucial to foster a space for thoughtful, informed analysis.

I invite readers to venture beyond the surface of eye-catching headlines and promises of instant wealth, to explore the subtleties and less-discussed truths of Bitcoin. This includes acknowledging its structural flaws that self-prevent Bitcoin itself from becoming what it aspired to be: a decentralized world currency.

I want readers to question why they are investing or believing in Bitcoin: is it because of the enthusiasm generated by more anecdotal or outright false success stories or a real understanding of what Bitcoin is and what it represents?

By planting this seed, I hope to contribute to a more reality-based dialog about Bitcoin and cryptocurrencies in general, not in hypothetical situations that are impossible to give. While not everyone will change their minds or take a critical view, encouraging such reflection and questioning their convictions would already be a significant achievement. So, while the book is not meant to convince Bitcoin's hardcore believers, I hope it does not at least foster even more hatred.

## ATTACKING BITCOIN IS NOT DEFENDING AN OLD-SCHOOL SYSTEM

Criticizing the Bitcoin system does not automatically imply a defense of traditional financial systems, which also present numerous problems and challenges. The objective of such a critique, in the context of this book, is to analyze in an objective and detailed way whether Bitcoin, with all its characteristics and peculiarities, represents a definitive solution to the problems inherent to the current financial system.

By questioning Bitcoin, we seek to understand whether this cryptocurrency can overcome the limitations and failures of the established financial system, such as lack of financial inclusion, inflation, corruption, banking crises, and manipulation by entities and governments. While Bitcoin was conceived as a decentralized, democratic alternative to the centralized financial system, it is essential to examine whether it can actually meet these aspirations.

This critical analysis is not intended to discredit Bitcoin's value or potential in the financial space, but rather to assess its effectiveness as a tool to address systemic flaws in the global financial framework. The intention is not to tear down the walls of the existing financial system, but to question whether Bitcoin, as it is currently constituted and used, can offer a viable and sustainable alternative - a spoiler: it cannot, and will not; not because of other agents or the current financial system, but on its own merits that impede its success.

It is important to distinguish between Bitcoin's theoretical potential and its actual performance. While in theory it offers many advantages, such as decentralization, security through cryptography and the blockchain network - which does have intrinsic value - and transparency of transactions, in practice it faces challenges such as price volatility, limited scalability, energy consumption from mining, and issues of accessibility and usability for the average user.

Moreover, criticism of Bitcoin should not be interpreted as a rejection of innovation or the search for alternatives to the conventional financial system. Rather, it is a question of raising one's hand and warning that, while the current financial system has plenty of downsides, the solution is not Bitcoin. It is vital to maintain this critical approach, and not to assume that any technological innovation, simply because it is new or disruptive or based on ideals, is automatically superior to existing systems.

The book's mission is to critically question whether Bitcoin represents the ultimate solution to the problems of the current financial system, without ignoring the flaws in the existing system. It is about understanding whether Bitcoin, with its advantages and disadvantages, can offer a fairer, more inclusive, and sustainable financial model for the future.

# THE REAL PROBLEM

# SLOWNESS AS ACHILLES HEEL

## IMPOSSIBLE TO IGNORE

In the world of cryptocurrencies, Bitcoin stands out as one of the most popular and used. As popular as it is slow. Bitcoin transactions have particularities that affect their speed and efficiency. A typical Bitcoin transaction, which in simple terms equates to a purchase, can take around 10 minutes to complete under the most basic validation process (1 token). This lapse is due to the time it takes to verify and record the transaction on the Bitcoin blockchain. Although this time may seem reasonable for some financial transactions, it poses not only significant challenges but also inability to enter its scalability of use as a currency. It is simply impossible to use Bitcoin in such an everyday situation as buying tea in a coffee shop; or, in general, buying anything and having to wait 10 minutes in a world where convenience is paramount above all else.

The scalability of Bitcoin as a means of payment faces serious issues due to this inherent slowness. For example, in a practical context such as a coffee shop, if a payment were made in Bitcoin, the customer would have to wait about 10 minutes for the transaction to be processed before receiving their order. This wait is multiplied with each additional customer in line, which could result in excessive waits for situations as simple as buying a tea. If you have three people in front of you, you are cursed. You will have to wait 30 minutes. Imagine the supermarket line. Not to mention other purchases where speed is even more key to the operation of the product or service. For example, imagine having to wait 10 minutes to cross a toll. Obviously, the key point is not just that you have to wait, it is, again, how many are in the queue and the accumulated wait. It does not make sense.

This slowness in processing is not solved simply by increasing the system's computing capacity, which highlights a fundamental problem in Bitcoin's architecture that limits its utility as a fast and efficient day-to-day currency.

## GOING INTO DETAIL

At the heart of the debate about Bitcoin's long-term viability lies a fundamental technical question that cannot be ignored: the slowness of its processing. This chapter carefully examines how the inherent slowness in confirming transactions in the Bitcoin network not only puts its scalability at risk, but also makes it impossible for it to function as an efficient global payment system.

The Bitcoin network, designed as a decentralized distributed accounting system, relies on blockchain technology to record transactions. However, its protocol sets an average time of 10 minutes to add a new block to the string. This design was intended to secure the network against malicious attacks and allow the synchronization of nodes across the network. However, this mechanism has created a significant bottleneck that limits the number of transactions the network can process per second.

That is, the intrinsic characteristic that makes Bitcoin a secure network - among other things - is the same that makes its large-scale triumph as a currency impossible.

Compared to traditional payment systems like Visa or MasterCard, which can handle thousands of transactions per second, Bitcoin pales in its ability to process between 4 to 7 transactions per second. This limitation becomes a critical issue when the demand for transactions increases, leading to delays and an increase in transaction rates, thus undermining Bitcoin's value proposition as an efficient and accessible payment system.

Again, the slowness in processing transactions directly affects Bitcoin scalability. Scalability, in the context of cryptocurrencies, refers to the ability of a network to grow and handle an increase in demand without compromising performance or security. For Bitcoin to become a global payment system, it must be able to handle transaction volumes comparable to those of established financial networks. That is, so that Bitcoin can be used as currency - hence its name 'cryptocurrency.'

The debate on how to improve Bitcoin scalability has been a constant in the community. Proposals such as increasing block sizes or implementing second-tier solutions such as the Lightning Network have emerged as viable solutions. However, these proposals have their own limitations and have not been implemented in a way that definitively solves the problem.

This slowness in transaction processing is an intrinsic problem of Bitcoin's current architecture. Unless significant changes are implemented in the network infrastructure, Bitcoin could remain a speculative asset rather than a revolutionary payment system. The problem is that this would require fundamental changes and the creation of BTC fora, and thus we would no longer be talking about Bitcoin but another cryptocurrency - to be simplified. Therefore, all those investments in BTC would be meaningless because now the appeal would be in another, more scalable cryptocurrency.

In the Bitcoin network, a transaction is considered confirmed when it is included in a block and it is added to the blockchain. The number of confirmations indicates how many blocks have been added to the blockchain after the block containing the transaction. The more confirmations a transaction has, the more secure it is considered, due to the increasing difficulty of altering the blockchain as new blocks are added.

Number of Confirmations Required

The number of confirmations required to validate a Bitcoin transaction varies depending on the level of security required by the receiver and the policy of the entity managing the wallet or platform:

A confirmation is usually sufficient for small or low-value transactions. A transaction with a confirmation is considered to have a minimal risk of being reversed. However, for more significant amounts, more confirmations are recommended.

Six confirmations are considered the industry standard for assuming a transaction is irreversible. This number is based on the premise that, after six blocks, the difficulty and cost of conducting a double-spending attack are prohibitively high for most attackers.

More than six confirmations may be required for very high value transactions or in security-critical situations. Some platforms or services require up to 30 confirmations to ensure maximum security, especially in environments that are particularly sensitive to the risk of double spending or attacks.

Confirmation modalities in the Bitcoin network vary mainly based on priority and transaction rates:

High priority transactions: Those with higher rates are confirmed faster because miners prioritize them to be included in the next block to be mined. This means that they can reach one or more confirmations in a shorter time.

Low priority transactions: If a transaction has a low rate, it might take longer to get the first confirmation, especially during periods of high network traffic. In these cases, a transaction can remain unconfirmed for hours or even days.

the number of confirmations required to validate a Bitcoin transaction depends on the level of security required by the receiver. For everyday transactions, a few confirmations may be sufficient, while for more significant fund movements or in high-risk environments, many more confirmations are preferred to ensure the irreversibility of the transaction.

Let us look at a schematic of the different confirmations in the Bitcoin network and their estimated mean times, based on the 10-minute interval it typically takes to mine a block.

These times are approximate and may vary depending on network congestion and transaction fees offered. Transactions with higher rates take precedence on the network and can be confirmed faster than transactions with lower rates. So in a linear fashion, we would have a scheme like this, where I insist, the first validation you need already takes about 10 minutes to process.

1 confirmation: estimated time: 10 minutes

Security: Low. Acceptable for low value transactions.

3 confirmations: estimated time: 30 minutes

Security: Moderate. Usually enough for small to medium transactions.

6 confirmations: estimated time 1 hour

Security: High. Industry standard for most transactions.

12 confirmations: estimated time 2 hours

Security: Very high. Used for higher value transactions.

30 confirmations: estimated time 5 hours

Security: Extremely high. Required for large transactions or on platforms that demand maximum security.

## THE COMPARISONS ARE ODIOUS

On the surface we have mentioned that some people consider BTC as a currency - hence the cryptocurrency - even though it is not yet used to buy anything. Others understand Bitcoin as a financial asset. Others understand Bitcoin as an alternative financial system. And others do not understand Bitcoin directly.

In any case, when comparing different assets and uses, we must be fair and compare the same cases. In an absurdity, it makes no sense to compare a $10 bill to a log, even if both can be burned. It is obvious, but at the same time there is a lot of bias involved in comparing a BTC use case to another type of financial asset in a different property. To cut a long story short, if we compare the slowness of BTC as a payment system, you should compare the speed of other systems as payment systems, not compare them with another of its functionalities.

When evaluating Bitcoin transaction speed versus other payment methods, it is critical to analyze the confirmation time along with the scale and context specific to each system. Bitcoin, as I have reiterated, requires about 10 minutes to get the first confirmation of a transaction, with a recommended total of 6 confirmations to ensure its security, adding up to about 60 minutes. Its capacity is limited to 4 to 7 transactions per second (tps), standing out for its high security, decentralized nature, and irreversibility.

By contrast, traditional payment systems such as credit cards, represented by Visa and MasterCard, provide instant confirmation for the approval of transactions, although the final settlement process can take from 1 to 3 days. These systems can handle approximately 65,000 tps, being widely accepted, with the possibility of reversal in case of fraud, and work centrally.

Bank transfers, on the other hand, such as those made over SWIFT, can have confirmation times ranging from a few hours to several days, depending on the banking network and international borders. The processing power of these transfers depends on each banking network, and although they are secure and widely used for cross-border transfers, they can be costly and time-consuming. Perfect, but irrelevant if we consider BTC as a bargaining chip.

Finally, electronic payment systems like PayPal and Venmo allow instant transactions between users of the same service, although transferring funds to bank accounts can take 1-3 days. The capacity of these systems is generally high for transactions between users, offering convenience and the possibility of reversal, although they may incur fees.

That is, with other properties that might be called into question - for example, centralization - if we adjust to speed, there are already other, more efficient solutions than Bitcoin.

## IMPLICATIONS IN ALL YOUR USE CASES

The examples below demonstrate that the slowness of Bitcoin processing is a significant obstacle to its mass adoption and functioning as an efficient global financial system. For Bitcoin to reach its revolutionary potential, it is imperative to address these challenges and their practical utility.

Imagine a scenario in which a customer tries to buy a coffee with Bitcoin. In an efficient payment system, the transaction would be approved almost instantaneously - that is, as it is now. However, due to Bitcoin's slowness, both the customer and the merchant must wait several minutes to confirm that the transaction has been added to the blockchain and is irreversible. This delay is impractical in a fast business environment where efficiency and speed are essential to customer flow and operational management.

In the case of buying high-value goods, such as a property or a car, the slowness in processing Bitcoin can generate uncertainty for both the buyer and the seller. Waiting for confirmation not only delays the deal, but also exposes both sides to volatility risks in the Bitcoin price. This waiting period can result in significant changes in the value of the transaction, potentially affecting the fairness of the agreement. True, this affects all transactions - even low-cost products but at the same time with perhaps tighter margins - but the more absolute amount - in the example, a car - the greater the change would be from volatility. But this point, the volatility, we will look at in more detail later.

For cryptocurrency investors and traders, speed in executing transactions can be crucial, especially in volatile markets. Slow Bitcoin processing limits traders' ability to take advantage of fast market opportunities or mitigate losses in market downturn situations. This disadvantage reduces the effectiveness of Bitcoin as a trading tool compared to faster cryptocurrencies or traditional trading systems. Paradoxically, the only current use is for speculative trading... but not 'high-speed trading' as is the case in other financial instruments such as the stock exchange.

While Bitcoin has been praised for its potential to facilitate international remittances by reducing transaction costs and time compared to traditional banking systems, the reality is that slow processing affects the most mundane operations undermining Bitcoin's competitive advantage in this sector.

## IT IS NOT SOLVED BY ADDING MORE COMPUTATION

Continuing with the analysis, it is crucial to understand that the slowness in processing Bitcoin transactions, far from being a mere technical obstacle, reflects a complexity inherent in its blockchain design. Often, one might think that increasing processing capacity, adding more computational power to the network, or increasing incentives to miners might be the solution. However, this perspective ignores the fundamental limitations and intentionally designed tradeoffs within the Bitcoin architecture.

The most obvious example of the consequences of this slowness is seen during peak demand. At times when interest in Bitcoin is growing exponentially, either due to fluctuations in the market or due to events that increase the visibility of cryptocurrencies, the network is saturated by a volume of transactions that exceeds its capacity. This results not only in longer wait times for the confirmation of transactions, but also in an exponential increase in transaction fees. For example, during the peak of cryptocurrency fever in late 2017, waiting times of hours and even days were recorded, along with commissions exceeding $50 per transaction in some cases.

Bitcoin's design incorporates a mechanism called Proof of Work (PoW), which is essential for its operation and security. This mechanism requires miners to use a lot of computational power to solve complex mathematical problems, in order to validate transactions and add them to the blockchain. The process is intentionally designed to be resource-intensive and slow as a security measure, to prevent tampering and network attacks.

Moreover, Bitcoin's decentralized nature means that any change in its structure, such as increasing the size of blocks to speed up transaction processing, requires widespread consensus among all network participants. Achieving this consensus is a complex task, as different actors may have divergent interests or concerns about the effects such changes might have on the security, decentralization, and integrity of the currency.

Therefore, slow processing is not simply a technical problem that can be solved by increasing processing power or hardware efficiency. It is an inherent feature of Bitcoin's blockchain design, deeply rooted in its commitment to security and decentralization. This design poses a fundamental dilemma: how to increase scalability without compromising the basic principles that make Bitcoin a decentralized, secure currency. Solving this dilemma remains one of the biggest challenges for the future of Bitcoin and cryptocurrencies in general.

The main proposals to solve the problem of Bitcoin transaction processing slowness and its limitations in scalability include increasing block size, implementing the Lightning Network, and adopting parallel blockchains or sidechains but all at the cost of 'stop talking about Bitcoin' and talk about 'something else.' It is at this time that backward compatibility and other factors become relevant.

Below we will look at these proposals along with the main reasons why they face difficulties in succeeding:

Increase block size

Proposal: Increasing the size of the blocks in the Bitcoin blockchain would allow to include more transactions in each block, accelerating the processing.

Limitations: More hardware and storage resources would be required to process and store larger blocks, which could exclude smaller miners and consolidate power in the hands of large node operators. In addition, this could increase block propagation time, affecting network security and decentralization. Not to mention the costs again: it may not be profitable for the miners that processing (for the energy costs) if the reward (the value of BTC) does not accompany to the same extent.

Lightning Network

Proposal: A second layer solution that creates payment channels between users, allowing almost instant transactions and extremely low costs, without the need to record all transactions on the main blockchain.

Limitations: Adoption of the Lightning Network has been slower than expected, partly due to technical complexity and usability challenges. In addition, there are concerns that it may create centralized payment systems and does not fully address the scalability issue for users who are not directly connected through an established channel. That is, giving up on fundamental aspects of Bitcoin – decentralization, security, and compatibility- which are the main differentials of the network.

Parallel Block Chains (Sidechains)

Proposal: Sidechains are independent blockchains that are connected to the main Bitcoin blockchain. They allow the transfer of assets between the main chain and the sidechain, offering a way to experiment with different block configurations and processing capabilities.

Limitations: Sidechains require the implementation of complex security mechanisms to avoid problems such as double spending and other attack vectors. In addition, its success depends on adoption and community support, and interoperability and security issues may arise that complicate its integration with the Bitcoin network. The same, to give up intrinsic aspects of Bitcoin and create other 'things' that are not Bitcoin and that, therefore, would need a separate book; because let us remember that the book focuses on the viability of BTC, not all cryptocurrencies... although we will talk about it in another chapter.

These proposals, while innovative and with the potential to improve Bitcoin's scalability, face significant challenges to their implementation and widespread acceptance. Concerns about security, centralization, technical complexity, and user adoption represent considerable obstacles that make it difficult for these solutions to succeed as definitive steps to solve Bitcoin's scalability problems.

# THAT ROLLER COASTER CALLED BITCOIN AND THE INSECURITY OF VOLATILITY

## HIGH VOLATILITY, LOW CONFIDENCE, ZERO ADOPTION

Bitcoin volatility is another crucial factor that discourages both consumers and businesses from adopting it as a currency. Imagine a situation where a consumer makes a purchase with a value of 0.1 BTC. If within the next few minutes or days the value of Bitcoin experiences a significant variation, it may be more beneficial for the consumer to return the purchased product to recover its 0.1 BTC, now increased in value, and possibly convert them to dollars or euros.

This scenario is not merely hypothetical, but reflects a reality where the fluctuation of the value of Bitcoin can have direct consequences on daily economic decisions, affecting the stability and predictability necessary for a currency to be considered reliable for regular transactions.

That is why, to this day, any business that says it accepts BTC, all it does is accept the conversion at that time of BTC to a currency. So, in reality, you are paying in EUR or USD converted to BTC and the same if you return the product. They do not return BTC to you, but the conversion of those EUR or USD into the new quote.

While volatility is not an inherent aspect of Bitcoin's design or structure, it has characterized its behavior in financial markets to date. This instability has been capitalized on by many for profit, especially in activities such as Day trading and speculation, where volatility can be exploited to generate significant financial returns in short periods of time. While volatility could theoretically decrease as the Bitcoin market matures and stabilizes, so far it has been a distinctive feature that has largely shaped the perception and adoption of Bitcoin, not only as an investment asset, but also undermined its potential use as a stable currency.

Not only does it undermine its potential as a currency, but high volatility also penalizes another supposed benefit: safe-haven value versus other assets.

Interestingly, to the extent that it lacks this high volatility, and therefore, it is no longer a magic bullet to get rich quickly or you can't speculate, many will stop looking at it attractive and disinvest in the cryptocurrency, it will lower the value and we will see that neither as a safe haven value nor as a currency - for the reasons already explained - will make any sense.

## GOING INTO DETAIL

Bitcoin has emerged as a disruptive phenomenon, challenging traditional notions of what constitutes a currency. However, its innovative character is accompanied by exceptional volatility, an aspect that has generated both fascination and critical concern. While not an intrinsic characteristic, the motivations behind and increasingly so, the volatility of BTC - or at least more than its use as a currency since it is non-existent - is linked, thus defining the user experience, but also raising fundamental questions about Bitcoin's long-term viability.

Bitcoin's volatility is palpable in its dramatic price fluctuations, where significant changes can occur within hours or even minutes. This phenomenon is not only a matter of interest for speculators and investors; it has profound implications for those looking for a stable currency in Bitcoin for everyday transactions. The essence of a currency, in traditional economic terms, is to serve as a medium of exchange, unit of account, and store of value. But Bitcoin's high volatility undermines these functions, especially when prices can vary enormously in short periods of time.

Take, for example, the perspective of a business that accepts Bitcoin as payment. Volatility can mean that the value of what has been received in Bitcoin can decrease (or increase) significantly in the time between the transaction and the time the business converts Bitcoin to a Fiat currency. This uncertainty hampers financial planning, pricing of goods or services, and can erode profit margins. For consumers, volatility turns using Bitcoin into a kind of gambling game, where the act of buying a simple item can result in an unintended monetary loss or gain due to price fluctuations.

Volatility also affects the perception of Bitcoin as a store of value. While some promote it as "digital gold," the reality is that stability is a critical component of any store of reliable value. Gold, for example, has maintained its value over time or increased in a controlled way - literally, designed like this - showing relative stability compared to Bitcoin. Bitcoin's wild price swings pose a significant risk to those seeking to preserve their capital overall, which may lead to questions about its suitability as a true safe-haven asset.

Moreover, Bitcoin's extreme volatility can be attributed to several factors, including its limited and fixed supply, rampant speculation, and its nascent adoption and integration into global financial systems. Unlike Fiat currencies, which are managed by central banks capable of adjusting the money supply to stabilize value, Bitcoin lacks a centralized control mechanism. This decentralization is both a strength and a weakness: while it provides freedom and autonomy from political or economic manipulation, it also means that there is no buffer against market volatility.

While volatility can offer lucrative opportunities for speculation, it undermines Bitcoin's ability to function effectively as a medium of exchange and store of value. Unless these issues are addressed, the uncertainty generated by Bitcoin volatility will continue to be a significant obstacle to its widespread adoption and long-term stability as a currency.

Imagine Alex, a freelance software developer who, attracted by the innovation and potential of cryptocurrencies, agrees with a new customer to receive their payment for a project in Bitcoin. The deal is simple: complete a specific job for 0.5 BTC. At the time of the deal, 0.5 BTC equals approximately $10,000, an attractive and fair sum for the work Alex has to do.

But Bitcoin's volatile nature soon begins to play a crucial role in this story. At the start of the project, the value of Bitcoin is at a peak, but as Alex moves forward in his work, the cryptocurrency market is experiencing a sharp decline. By the time Alex completes the project, the value of 0.5 BTC has fallen to $6,000, representing a significant loss in the expected value of his compensation.

Alex is in a delicate position. Although he has technically received the agreed amount of Bitcoin, the real value of his work has been drastically reduced in terms of purchasing power. This change affects your financial planning and your perception of the value of working with cryptocurrency-based payments.

The situation becomes even more complicated if the value of Bitcoin rises after Alex has converted his 0.5 BTC to a Fiat currency to cover his expenses. If the value soars to $15,000 for 0.5 BTC after conversion, Alex might feel that he not only lost by selling at the low point, but also missed an additional profit opportunity.

This scenario highlights the risks associated with Bitcoin volatility for individuals who rely on cryptocurrencies for their income. Although Bitcoin prices can rise, sometimes benefiting workers, the unpredictability of the market can result in financially unfavorable situations, underscoring the importance of risk management strategies and careful consideration when accepting cryptocurrencies as a form of payment in labor agreements.

Simply and simply, would you agree to collect your salary at BTC without knowing how much it will be worth in 30 days?

The uncertainty generated by Bitcoin volatility is not only a problem for individuals and businesses, but also poses macroeconomic challenges. Governments and financial institutions, for example, find it difficult to integrate Bitcoin into established economic systems because of its unpredictability. This volatility prevents Bitcoin from being considered a reliable medium for international transactions and value reserves at the government or institutional level. Moreover, drastic swings in Bitcoin's value can influence economic decisions, affecting investment, consumption, and saving policies.

The decentralized nature of Bitcoin, though one of its greatest attractions, complicates the picture further. In the absence of a central entity that can intervene to stabilize the price, the Bitcoin market is at the mercy of supply and demand dynamics, exacerbated by speculation and reaction to global developments.

Bitcoin's sensitivity to news and events, from government regulations to changes in public perception, reinforces its volatility. Importantly, this volatility does not only affect Bitcoin holders. Bitcoin miners, too, are more or less incentivized by the currency's own value. It has a ripple effect on the cryptocurrency market in general, as many other digital currencies and tokens are linked or influenced by Bitcoin fluctuations. Thus, Bitcoin instability can cause widespread uncertainty in the cryptocurrency market, affecting investors, companies, and regulators.

To mitigate these effects, some potential solutions have emerged, such as stablecoins, which are tied to more stable assets like the US dollar, gold, or a basket of currencies, thereby providing a haven against volatility. However, these instruments bring their own challenges and risks, and do not address the underlying problem of volatility in Bitcoin itself.

As long as Bitcoin continues to exhibit significant levels of volatility, its role as a globally accepted currency and stable storage medium will be questionable. Volatility is not a technical feature of Bitcoin; but it is a manifestation of its unique position as a speculative asset. Resolving this dichotomy (currency vs speculation) is critical to Bitcoin's future and its potential to transform the global financial system sustainably.

As we can see, it is difficult to resolve when both positions are self-reinforcing.

Víctor de la Fuente

## THE MYTH OF DECENTRALIZATION

The theoretical idea of decentralization, which is central to Bitcoin's philosophy, turns out to be, at least, partially questionable when one looks at the operational reality of the network. In practice, considerable concentration is perceived in two principal areas: Bitcoin possession and the mining process. Although Bitcoin was designed to operate as a decentralized currency, where no single entity has total control, the accumulation of substantial amounts of Bitcoin in the hands of a small number of individuals (whales) or entities has led to a situation where wealth and therefore power within the network, are remarkably centralized.

This concentration of possession not only contradicts the principle of decentralization, but also raises concerns about market manipulation and the disproportionate influence of certain actors on the price and stability of Bitcoin.

On the other hand, Bitcoin mining, which is critical for network maintenance and security, also shows signs of centralization. Although theoretically anyone with the right equipment can participate in mining, the reality is that the cost and efficiency needed to compete effectively have led to the creation and domination of large mining farms and consortia dedicated to this goal.

These groups have a massive processing capacity, which allows them to have a significant influence on the verification and block creation process. This centralization in mining can compromise the security and fairness of the network, which is far from the original vision of the democratic network that Bitcoin intended to be.

## THEORETICALLY...

Bitcoin is considered a decentralized currency because of its design and operation, which allow it to operate independently of central authorities, such as central banks or governments.

Very brutally, Bitcoin functions as a P2P network, where transactions are made directly between users without the need for intermediaries. This structure allows anyone anywhere in the world to participate in the network, contributing to its maintenance and operation.

At the heart of Bitcoin is blockchain - whose system does have value - which is nothing more than a public and distributed digital ledger that records all transactions. Each block in the chain contains a number of transactions, and once a block is added to the chain, the information it contains is considered immutable and permanent because it is distributed throughout the network. This ensures transparency of all transactions and resists any manipulation or hacking as it is 'impossible' to alter blocks already established on the distributed network.

The creation of new blocks and network security are maintained through a process called mining. Miners use computational power to solve complex mathematical problems, and the first miner to solve the problem and validate the block receives a reward in Bitcoin - hence the value of Bitcoin is key to the miners' profitability versus the energy costs in running that computational processing. This process, known as Proof of Work (PoW), ensures a decentralized consensus on the state of blockchain.

Bitcoin is open source software, which means its source code is publicly available and can be reviewed, audited, and modified by anyone - to create countless other cryptocurrencies. This promotes transparency and allows the community of users and developers to actively participate in the evolution and improvement of the network.

Unlike fiat currencies, which are issued and regulated by government entities or central banks, Bitcoin does not have a central authority that controls their issuance or value. Bitcoin issuance is predetermined by the network algorithm and limited to 21 million units, which eliminates the possibility of arbitrary inflation.

Although all Bitcoin transactions are public and can be viewed by anyone on the blockchain, user identities remain anonymous. Bitcoin addresses, which are alphanumeric strings, do not contain directly identifiable personal information, which provides a level of privacy to users.

For all these reasons, Bitcoin is considered a decentralized currency, as its design and operation eliminate the need for central authorities, foster transparency, and community participation, and ensure that transaction control and verification is distributed through a global network of users and miners.

## IN PRACTICE

In practice, as we will see, it is that both on both sides - mining and maintenance of the Bitcoin network as well as on Bitcoin holders - there is a high concentration of players.

The concentration of Bitcoin mining has varied significantly over the years, with notable changes in geographic distribution due to regulatory, economic, and technological factors. It is interesting to see the development of mining over time to see how geopolitical factors and costs have influenced more than the value and adoption of Bitcoin itself and how it affects, de facto, the supposed democratization and decentralization of the currency.

Until mid-2021, China dominated Bitcoin mining, controlling roughly 65% to 75% of the global hashrate. However, this dominance was drastically reduced after the Chinese government implemented bans and severe restrictions on cryptocurrency mining in the region.

Following restrictions in China, the U.S. experienced a boom in Bitcoin mining. By the end of 2021 and the beginning of 2022, the US was estimated to have taken the lead in Bitcoin mining, accounting for about 35% to 40% of the global hashrate. This growth is due to the migration of miners from China and investment in mining infrastructure on U.S. territory.

Kazakhstan also became a major hub for Bitcoin mining, accounting for about 18% of the global hashrate sometime in 2021. However, it faces challenges due to regulatory and energy supply issues.

Russia has maintained a significant presence in Bitcoin mining, albeit with less dominance than China or the US. Russia was estimated to control about 11% of the world's hashrate in certain periods of 2021, but due to international blockades due to the war in Ukraine and Russian opacity it is difficult to quantify or make more recent estimates.

Canada, with its cold climate and relatively cheap and sustainable energy sources, has attracted Bitcoin miners, although its share of the global hashrate is considerably lower compared to the countries mentioned above. Other countries such as Iceland, Norway, and some in the Eastern Europe and Central Asia region have also attracted mining activities due to advantages such as cold weather and access to affordable renewable energy.

It is important to mention that the dynamics of Bitcoin mining continue to evolve rapidly, influenced by factors such as changes in regulatory policies, availability of energy resources and development of mining technology. Therefore, country-by-country mining concentration statistics may change over time, reflecting the fluctuating state of the global cryptocurrency mining market.

Instead, fluctuations in the acquisition and safeguarding of Bitcoins as a financial asset answer different questions but also raise some alarms about their actual decentralization.

The concentration of Bitcoin ownership among so-called whales, or large holders, is a widely discussed topic in the cryptocurrency ecosystem. Although it is more difficult to get accurate statistics on Bitcoin property distribution due to the anonymous and decentralized nature of blockchain, several studies and analyzes of blockchain data have provided some estimates.

It is estimated that a small portion of Bitcoin addresses controls a substantial portion of the total Bitcoin in circulation. For example, reports have suggested that roughly 2% of addresses own more than 95% of all Bitcoin. However, this analysis can be misleading, since a single address can represent a cryptocurrency exchange - for example, Coinbase - or a custodian service that owns Bitcoin on behalf of thousands or millions of users - which in any case, remains the sole holder of the BTC and not the users themselves, although surely they are not aware and believe that they are real holders of the BTC.

I will make a point at this point to make it even clearer: many exchanges are in practice the real custodians of the digital asset at the expense of users not being aware of it and believing they own that digital asset. What happens if an Exchange or custodian goes bankrupt? Users do not have any rights or access to the asset they thought they owned - in this case BTC - and therefore lose it. This case is not a hypothetical example but has already happened on numerous occasions with digital assets such as NFTs and also with Bitcoin itself and several famous exchanges, one of them: Quadriga.

Users or people - or even more accurately, addresses - considered as "whales" are those who own substantial amounts of Bitcoin. These addresses often belong to wealthy individuals, investment institutions, or large trading platforms and custody services. The movement of funds from and to these addresses can have significant impacts on the Bitcoin market due to the volume of their transactions; remember that 2% handle 95% of BTCs.

Cryptocurrency exchanges play a key role in Bitcoin concentration, as many users prefer to keep their funds on these platforms to facilitate trading and access to other services. Bitcoin's combined balances on major exchanges represent a sizable portion of the total Bitcoin in circulation.

With the growing interest of institutional investors in Bitcoin, there has been an increase in the concentration of ownership in entities that can acquire substantial amounts of Bitcoin. Hedge funds, investment companies and corporations have begun to include Bitcoin in their portfolios, contributing to the concentration of ownership.

While it increases risk or transparency for those small investors who are not the real custodians of those assets, I will not repeat myself again.

Although Bitcoin's network is decentralized, the distribution of its ownership is not. This concentration creates a market dynamic where Bitcoin price movements are significantly influenced by the decisions of a relatively small number of participants; a well-known evil.

The concentration of power among the main Bitcoin miners and holders reveals an irony in cryptocurrency: despite its decentralized and democratic design, in practice, it operates under a form of unofficial centralization.

To address these problems, reforms in Bitcoin's structure that encourage further decentralization are required. Proposals such as improving the protocol to reduce the advantage of large mining farms, encouraging a more equitable distribution of Bitcoin, and implementing technologies that reduce the power of large miners, are essential to align Bitcoin's operational reality with its founding principles.

But if we implement these reforms, we will no longer talk about Bitcoin but surely about 'something else' - one of so many forks or alt-coins.

## WHAT WILL HAPPEN IF THERE ARE NO MINERS TO KEEP THE GOLD?

I f Bitcoin mining ceases to be profitable for miners, we could witness a number of significant consequences that would affect both the stability of the network and the overall dynamics of the cryptocurrency market. The profitability of Bitcoin mining depends on several factors, including Bitcoin price, energy cost, mining hardware efficiency and block rewards.

The outflow of miners could lead to further centralization of mining in those actors who can afford to continue operating, possibly because they have access to cheaper energy or have invested in hardware - I don't want to get into the mad rush that the crypto world experienced a few years ago with Nvidia graphics cards or the latest race for chips focused on mining or AI. This centralization ironically contradicts Bitcoin's theoretical decentralization principle and concentrating power in the hands of a few, which, being sensational, would affect governance and network integrity.

The Bitcoin network automatically adjusts the difficulty of mining to ensure that the average time to mine a block - and stays at about 10 minutes in case it did not seem slow enough. If many miners are removed from the network, the difficulty of mining should lessen to compensate for the loss of hash power and maintain that block creation frequency or make it slower - yes, even slower. However, this adjustment may not be sufficient to maintain the profitability of mining if the Bitcoin price does not hold or increases in proportion to operating costs.

In the long term, the lack of profitability in mining could impact the development and adoption of Bitcoin. Fewer miners and a reduced hash rate could lead to slower transaction times and increase Bitcoin price volatility.

In addition, it could affect the perception of Bitcoin as a safe and reliable asset, which is fundamental to its value and adoption as a store of value and medium of exchange.

Much less likely is that if Bitcoin mining becomes economically unviable, many miners might choose to turn off their equipment and quit the activity. A significant decrease in the hash rate could make the network more vulnerable to attacks, such as the 51% attack, where a malicious actor could theoretically gain control of most of the hash power and manipulate the blockchain for its benefit. But, in fairness, this is virtually unlikely.

To simplify, mining Bitcoins ceases to be profitable when the value of the BTC drops - remember that the reward of mining BTC is the BTC itself - or if operating costs - mostly electricity and water - exceed revenues.

**THEORETICALLY...**

Bitcoin mining faces several challenges that could make it economically unviable in the future, and these challenges are intrinsically linked to the structure and design of the Bitcoin system. For a change, it is not one, but multiple arguments that put Bitcoin mining at risk, and, at the same time, put at risk the potency of the argument since I am convinced that each of them has its counterargument and will continue to not convince blind believers.

The Bitcoin halving event, which occurs roughly every four years, halves the reward miners receive for adding a new block to the blockchain. This design aims to control inflation and emulate the progressive depletion of a natural resource such as gold. As rewards decline, mining profitability declines, unless there is a corresponding increase in Bitcoin value.

Competitiveness and Technology: Bitcoin's mining difficulty is automatically adjusted to keep block creation time at an average of 10 minutes. As more miners join the grid and mining technology becomes more efficient, the difficulty increases, requiring more computational power and therefore more investment and spending on electricity to maintain the same likelihood of successfully mining a block.

Bitcoin mining is an energy intensive process. Energy cost is a critical factor in the profitability of mining. With increased awareness of climate change and pressure to reduce energy consumption from non-renewable sources, miners may face higher energy costs and stricter regulations, affecting profitability.

In addition, as I mentioned, the profitability of Bitcoin mining is directly influenced by the market price of Bitcoin. High volatility can result in periods of high profitability followed by times when costs exceed revenues. This financial uncertainty may deter long-term investment in mining infrastructure.

The trend towards centralization in large mining farms, due to economies of scale, can marginalize small or individual miners, reducing competition and increasing the vulnerability of the network to centralized points of failure or manipulation. Although I insist, the vulnerability of the Bitcoin network is the least of its problems and I do not want to mention it even as an argument.

In the very long term, new technologies like quantum computing could change the current mining landscape; though, to be fair, quantum computing could bring even more significant changes in cybersecurity and perhaps in the blockchain network itself.

In any case, more tangible and short-term regulatory changes, especially in environmental terms, could affect the operation and cost of mining.

If not one separately, but also the combination of these factors suggests that, without adjustments in the Bitcoin mining economy or significant increases in the value of Bitcoin, mining activity could face serious profitability challenges in the future.

Even greater consolidation is a byproduct of the incentives behind the capitalist system itself that permeates not only Bitcoin but society. So Bitcoin is closer to succumbing to capitalism and being absorbed by it than it is to transforming the financial system but to adopting all its ills - the ills of capitalism.

## UNDER THE SHADOW OF A PONZI SCHEME

Bitcoin volatility, while making it attractive to speculators, carries the risk of fostering a pyramid-like dynamic. Speculators, lured by the possibility of quick profits, may become enthusiastic promoters of the asset, not necessarily because of a belief in its intrinsic value or long-term utility - questioned numerous times in the previous pages - but because of the financial interests at stake. This situation creates a cycle in which the value of Bitcoin is maintained or increased, not by its adoption as a currency or by its efficiency in solving financial problems, but by the continuous investment and promotion of those who seek to benefit from fluctuations in its price.

You can make money in Bitcoin, yeah. If it is at the expense of more capital - more people being cheated - or making money by chance from their Day trading volatility like playing in the casino, go for it. In any case, first, be well informed - with this book and so many others - and second, be honest with yourself and others.

### UNMOUNTING THE PYRAMID

Bitcoin, the pioneering cryptocurrency that promised to revolutionize the global financial system, is often at the center of a heated debate about its nature and economic sustainability. One strong criticism directed at him is the perception that he operates, or at least resembles, a pyramid scheme. This criticism is based on the fact that the value of Bitcoin seems to be more influenced by the amount of capital and the number of participants that enter the system, than by its real utility as a currency - non-existent. Here we delve into this critical perspective, examining the relationship between the flow of new investors, the rise in Bitcoin's value and its real-world functionality.

In a pyramid scheme, the financial return for previous participants depends directly on the steady flow of new participants. Similarly, Bitcoin's value has shown a tendency to increase with the entry of new investors and the capital they bring - and all the rumors, sensationalism, etc. that it brings with it - rather than traditional economic and utilitarian fundamentals. At what point did we think a cryptocurrency would want to act as a currency? Naive.

During Bitcoin price rallies, the narrative often focuses on the expectation of future price increases and the promise of high returns for early investors, rather than discussing the growth in its adoption as a currency for regular transactions. In the future we will adopt BTC as a currency; in the meantime... Paradoxically, the longer it takes for BTC to be adopted as a currency, the more likely it will never be used as such.

Extreme volatility in Bitcoin's price, with rapid boom-bust cycles, reinforces the perception that its value is decoupled from practical use - not because it is being used more or is being unused. Attracted by the promise of rapid wealth, investors often enter the market not with the intention of using Bitcoin as a medium of exchange, but with the hope that its value will continue to rise, allowing it to be sold at a higher price in the future. This speculative mindset can create a cycle in which Bitcoin's price is artificially inflated, based on expectations rather than its intrinsic value as a financial tool.

Whoever wants to argue that there is value simply as a speculative asset, I find that fantastic. At the same time, do not try to mask it with other alleged functionalities that, as we have seen, are difficult to scale.

Moreover, the focus on Bitcoin accumulation and retention, in the hope of long-term appreciation, contradicts the idea of a currency designed to be spent and used in everyday transactions. The reluctance to spend Bitcoin due to the expectation that its value will rise, known as the "austerity paradox," limits its functionality as a currency and encourages behavior reminiscent of that of participants in a pyramid scheme, where accumulating and waiting for new investors to boost value become the dominant strategy.

And because that is the dominant strategy, the incentives for the narrative in all media to be that way, and therefore not to fall the house of cards - allusion also to gambling - make it more like a pyramid scheme.

However, it is crucial to distinguish between the characteristics of a classic pyramid scheme and the functioning of Bitcoin. Unlike a pyramid scheme, where returns are generated exclusively from the investment of new entrants, Bitcoin has a limited supply and its output declines over time, which theoretically should increase in value if demand remains constant or increases. In addition, Bitcoin provides a decentralized and transparent infrastructure that does not rely on a central entity that promotes investment or recruits new entrants.

The problem is that all the cycles, difficulties, trends and how we want to express them do not respond to that intrinsic functioning yet but to mere speculation on the part of everyone.

The influence of influencers and celebrities on the perception and value of Bitcoin cannot be underestimated. These individuals, along with current holders who own substantial amounts of Bitcoin, have an inherent incentive to promote cryptocurrency as an ideal asset, thereby boosting their own financial profit. This phenomenon adds another layer of complexity to the already intricate dynamics of the Bitcoin market, and deserves a detailed analysis to understand its implications on the perception and stability of Bitcoin's value.

Influencers and celebrities, with their audiences and the ability to shape public opinion, plus media where they care less about the truth and more about clickbait, play a crucial role in the Bitcoin narrative. By becoming a sponsor of BTC or any cryptocurrency exchange, they can trigger waves of interest and investment activity, often resulting in significant increases in the price of Bitcoin and thus in their own profit as holders of BTC or alt-coins... to obviously, then sell them.

For example, if a celebrity or certain figure, say Elon Musk, with millions of followers on social media speaks positively about Bitcoin or Dogecoin, this can drive up the price and revalue all of their wealth. Put plainly, this conflict of interest creates an inherent incentive for everyone on the network to raise more capital - people. So as popular as Bitcoin is and as accepted, it will not deprive you of a pyramid scheme — the largest in the world — but a pyramid scheme like any other pyramid scheme.

This dynamic is exacerbated by the fact that many of these public figures invest significantly in Bitcoin, cryptocurrencies, or exchanges, which means they have much to gain from their appreciation. In addition, as public figures, their investment, and support for Bitcoin can be seen as a trusted sponsor, encouraging their followers and the general public to invest as well. Although, for them, the percentage that he represents of his patrimony, except perhaps of Elon Musk, is derisory and relatively less than the percentage of all those who want to convince.

This incentive, as I say, does not only affect influencers and celebrities but is also applicable to all Bitcoin holders. Obviously not only will no one accept that he has been deceived, but he will also justify his position - dismantled in the book - and, worse, he will try to convince the more people the better to be able to revalue his operation.

For all these reasons, the discussion around Bitcoin is usually quite passionate - toxic.

But this steady and sometimes aggressive promotion raises doubts about long-term sustainability - though there is still much to swindle the world. If Bitcoin's value is significantly inflated by perception and speculation, it could be vulnerable to severe corrections if confidence declines or circumstances change.

The interaction between influencers, celebrities, Bitcoin holders and the general market highlights a feedback loop where promotion increases value, benefiting promoters and leaving Bitcoin in a perpetual state of speculation and volatility. This cycle can divert attention from the practical utility and actual adoption of Bitcoin as currency and payment system, as well as prevent it precisely because of that narrative, thus questioning the legitimacy of its perceived value and long-term stability.

The problem is that these counterarguments are also questioned both theoretically and practically, so there is no choice but to conclude what many do not want to recognize: if it resembles a pyramid scheme, in part acts as such, there is no extension of use, then perhaps...

Víctor de la Fuente

## USE CASES AND ACTUAL USE CASES ARE TWO TOTALLY DIFFERENT THINGS

The difference between theoretical use cases and actual use of Bitcoin has profound implications for its future development and adoption. This gap highlights not only expectations versus reality, but also the challenges and obstacles Bitcoin faces in reaching its full potential.

Use cases refer to the theoretical or hypothetical possibilities of how a technology can be applied. In the Bitcoin arena, use cases include potentials as a medium of exchange, store of value, or even as a tool of financial inclusion are essentially scenarios designed to show how Bitcoin could transform various aspects of the economy and society. For example, there is talk of Bitcoin as an alternative to fiat currencies, a safe haven against inflation, or a solution to facilitate international remittances more efficiently and cheaply.

Actual use, on the other hand, refers to the practical implementation and effective adoption of technology in everyday situations. It is the tangible manifestation of how technology is currently being used in people's daily lives and business operations. In the case of Bitcoin, real use involves looking at how it is being used in real transactions, the extent of its adoption as a payment method, or its integration into traditional financial systems. Although Bitcoin was conceived as a decentralized payment system, its actual use has evolved in ways that are often seen more as a speculative investment asset than as a currency in everyday use.

The discrepancy between use cases and actual use of Bitcoin is significant and revealing. While use cases paint a picture of what Bitcoin might be able to do, actual use shows what it is actually doing. This distinction is crucial to understanding the real value of Bitcoin and its impact on the financial and economic world.

For example, whenever there is news based on the 'infinite' number of transactions made with BTC, it is perceived that its actual use is becoming more widespread. Few argue that most of these transactions are inbred between BTC holders or between cryptocurrencies, not as 'real' uses of BTC as a currency or financial asset.

Another example. Although Bitcoin's ability to democratize financial access is being promoted, it is currently difficult for the average person to access and its impact is relative. This promise to democratize finance through technologies such as Bitcoin or other digital wallets means making these assets accessible and understandable to the general public, not just those with advanced technical knowledge.

Currently, access to these technologies is still perceived as "techy" or too technical, which poses significant barriers for the average user. This level of technical complexity can alienate many people, thereby preventing mass adoption of these technologies.

When we talk about democratization in the Bitcoin context, we are talking about the ability to provide equitable and easy access to the financial and cultural benefits these technologies promise. This means not only providing the necessary infrastructure, but also ensuring that the user experience is intuitive, secure, and free from unnecessary technical obstacles. In order to achieve true democratization, it is essential that anyone, regardless of their technical experience, can use these technologies without difficulty.

Currently, interacting with Bitcoin requires navigating a number of technical steps that can be daunting for many. From the configuration of a digital wallet, the understanding of private and public keys, to the execution of transactions and the understanding of market fluctuations, all these elements present a high degree of technical complexity, especially for populations that, in general, lack basic financial culture. Moreover, the language used in the cryptocurrency space is full of jargon that can be confusing and intimidating for newcomers.

For Bitcoin to become a truly democratizing tool, simplifying access and user experience is essential. This could involve the development of more user-friendly interfaces, accessible education and learning resources, and customer support. In addition, it is important that clear standards and regulations are in place to protect users from fraud and ensure transparency and fairness on these platforms.

If even advanced users do not master or care about terms such as digital asset custody, asking an average user to use a digital wallet, in the current state of development, is not only utopian but also irresponsible.

All this without counting segments of the population more vulnerable by different sociodemographic aspects. If older people currently have accessibility issues when it comes to apps and digital banking, imagine what would happen to digital wallets.

Digital wallets that, with all their advantages, reload all their responsibility on the user: from basic aspects such as not losing the key to controlling possible fraudulent movements.

You will more or less like centralization vs. decentralization, but certain aspects of centralization protect the user from potential scams.

As long as access to Bitcoin remains too technical and complex, its potential to democratize global finance will be limited. Mass adoption depends on making these technologies accessible, understandable, and usable to the general public, not just to those with advanced technical knowledge. Only then can Bitcoin achieve its promise of economically empowering a global and diverse audience.

And while Bitcoin use cases open the door to a world of possibilities, real use provides a basis for assessing its effectiveness and practical adoption in today's economy. The gap between these two concepts can serve as a critical indicator of Bitcoin's maturity as a technology and its acceptance in the mass market.

For now, the imagination and speculation win that real use... unless real use is purely speculative.

# EL SALVADOR, AN OASIS WITHOUT BITCOIN

The adoption of Bitcoin in El Salvador has been a topic of debate and analysis since the country adopted it as legal tender in September 2021. Although the Salvadoran government has promoted the use of Bitcoin with the aim of boosting the economy, attracting investment, and reducing the costs of remittances, the reality is quite different.

According to media reports and various analyzes, a sizable number of businesses in El Salvador do not accept Bitcoin, preferring to stick with traditional fiat currencies such as the US dollar, which is also legal tender in the country.

The reasons behind the reluctance include fluctuation in the value of Bitcoin, the complexity of the technology, lack of adequate infrastructure and widespread skepticism about the long-term benefits of its use. Moreover, although the government has implemented measures such as the creation of a national digital wallet (Chivo Wallet) and has offered incentives such as Bitcoin credits to citizens who use it, the acceptance is far from universal, and has even generated rejection - obvious - among a large part of the population.

The adoption of Bitcoin in El Salvador presents a complex scenario, with a divergence between the government's vision and the operational reality on the ground.

True, in the very long run, the adoption of Bitcoin, and especially in a scenario in which the dollar is not associated with oil - or is, at long last, replaced by other materials and energies - may attack the status quo of the dollar as a global currency. Until then, actions like those in El Salvador are more anecdotal and superficial than significant.

For now, it is nothing but a PR action.

## ALT-COINS: ALTERNATIVES TO NOTHING

The book addresses Bitcoin not only as an independent financial entity, but also as the paradigm of all cryptocurrencies, highlighting its position as the most influential - the rest of alt-coins are simply followers of the trend marked by BTC except perhaps Ethereum. This preeminence of Bitcoin in the cryptocurrency space is largely due to being the first and having significant success early by getting a critical mass of early adopters - myself included - without any fork or alt-coin calling into question the hegemony of BTC, not even ETH.

Bitcoin has become synonymous with cryptocurrencies in the collective consciousness and in financial markets, establishing itself as the standard against which all other cryptocurrencies are measured. Its value and recognition go beyond its technical characteristics, building on its ability to attract and maintain a broad and diverse user and believer base. This strength of Bitcoin derives not only from its technology, but also from its history. Its first advantage in the market was precisely to be the pioneer, and with it, the symbolism and idealism behind the innovative disruption - we will not deny that.

Ethereum and other Bitcoin forums have introduced significant improvements, such as smart contracts, faster transaction speeds, and more efficient or greener consensus mechanisms. But these technological advances have not been enough to eclipse Bitcoin's status as the de facto leading cryptocurrency. Bitcoin's influence on the market is evident in how fluctuations in its price affect the crypto market in general; alt-coins tend to follow Bitcoin's trend, rising when it rises and falling when it falls, which demonstrates Bitcoin's centrality in the crypto ecosystem.

The relationship between Bitcoin and alt-coins can be seen as one of leadership and tracking, where Bitcoin acts as the barometer of the crypto market. Although technologically some alt-coins may be superior, they lack the same weight and influence on the market. Bitcoin's prominence is based on its widespread acceptance, the perceived security of its time-tested network, and its ability to represent the ideal of a cryptocurrency in many people's minds.

If Bitcoin remains the central pillar of interest and investment in the cryptocurrency space, alt-coins will remain largely trackers of its trend, regardless of their technological merits. This dynamic underscore the importance of perception, trust, and history in the cryptocurrency economy, where Bitcoin continues to be the emblematic figure and reference point for the sector as a whole.

The argument that the criticisms applied to Bitcoin are invalid if applied to Dogecoin or other cryptocurrencies is a fallacy because it incorrectly assumes that all cryptocurrencies must be evaluated with the same set of criteria without considering their specific contexts, purposes, and mechanics. This perspective ignores the fundamental differences in the design, adoption, technology, and market of each cryptocurrency.

Comparing Bitcoin with Dogecoin (or any other alt-coin) and suggesting that one's problems invalidate or justify the other's is akin to contrasting the real estate systems of two different countries, like the UK and Spain, without considering their respective economic, legal, and market particularities. Each real estate system has its own challenges and dynamics that are the result of a complex web of historical, geographic, economic, and regulatory factors specific to each country.

In the context of cryptocurrencies, each currency was created with different objectives and under different premises. Bitcoin was launched as a decentralized currency intended to be a medium of exchange and a store of value. Dogecoin, on the other hand, started out as a meme cryptocurrency, and although it has gained popularity and acceptance, its original purpose and market mechanics are different from Bitcoin's. For example, Dogecoin has an inflationary supply (no currency ceiling), which affects its economy differently compared to Bitcoin's fixed supply.

The criticisms or problems identified in Bitcoin, such as its scalability, volatility, energy consumption in mining, or its partial centralization, should be understood in the context of its design, use and evolution. Applying these same flashpoints to Dogecoin or other cryptocurrencies results in a misinformed and potentially misleading comparison - and so I will not make one.

That is, the book is focused on Bitcoin as a representation of cryptocurrencies - for what it represents - but it does not mean that all arguments apply equally to the rest of cryptocurrencies. In fact, one of the arguments in favor of Bitcoin is its knowledge by the mainstream - although its access is difficult - while the rest of cryptocurrencies, perhaps technically better - lacks even recognition by users and therefore, hardly critical mass to become a currency or asset of value.

Bitcoin's influence on the crypto market and the financial system in general are exponentially greater compared to most other cryptocurrencies. Thus, the Bitcoin-directed criticisms not only address technical or market issues, but also broader concerns about the integration of cryptocurrencies into the global financial system and their effect on various economic and social aspects.

Coins that, by the way, we do not question, but sensationally speaking, I doubt the world needs hundreds of other cryptocurrencies. So the success of alt-coins is scarce because I do not foresee a future where not one - Bitcoin - and even less dozens of alternative currencies will be used.

In short, to argue that Bitcoin's problems are invalid because they can also be applied to Dogecoin or other cryptocurrencies is a fallacy that fails to recognize the intrinsic differences between these currencies. It is essential to evaluate each cryptocurrency in its own context, considering its purpose, functioning and the implications of its unique features. And I am not going to go in and evaluate every one of them.

In an absurd comparison, I will be able to agree or disagree with a cryptocurrency. Then, I will disagree or have a view on BTC and in general of alt-coins but I do not need to evaluate each of them to get a general idea of the validity of the arguments. For example, if I were an atheist, I do not need to prove or convince myself of every religion — monotheistic or polytheistic — and question every one of those gods, I just need to philosophize about the existence of god to reject the concept of god; not of every one of them. Ditto with BTC.

At the same time, invalidating arguments against Bitcoin by alluding to another cryptocurrency that has solved them is biased, to say the least. If we have established that the actual use of the most important cryptocurrency is scarce or non-existent, it is not worth developing the real use of that supposedly alternative currency that does solve the x problem concerning Bitcoin. If the argument that many crypto gurus rely on is mass adoption and mass consensus, that same argument goes against any alt-coin whose mainstream use is - and will be - zero.

## THE EXAMPLE OF SLOWNESS

While Bitcoin stands out for its security and decentralized character, it is relatively slow and limited in capacity when compared to traditional payment methods and some other cryptocurrencies. We are not gonna do any more blood about it.

Alternatives such as Ethereum, Ripple and Litecoin show that it is possible to offer faster and more scalable transaction systems, although each presents distinctive characteristics and compromises between speed, security, and decentralization.

Ethereum is characterized by a confirmation time of approximately 15 seconds per block, and it is recommended to obtain up to 12 confirmations to ensure greater security, which would add about 3 minutes in total. Its current capacity is around 30 transactions per second (tps), but a significant increase is anticipated with future upgrades, such as Ethereum 2.0. What distinguishes Ethereum, besides its speed, are its smart contract capabilities, which make it somewhat faster than Bitcoin and maintain its decentralized nature.

On the other hand, Ripple (XRP) shows impressive performance in terms of speed with a confirmation time of only 4 to 5 seconds and a processing capacity of 1,500 tps. Its focus is primarily on facilitating fast and cheap banking transactions, although this involves partial centralization, an aspect that sets it apart from many other cryptocurrencies.

Litecoin, by comparison, offers a confirmation time of approximately 2.5 minutes per block, with a capacity to process around 56 tps. Although based on Bitcoin, Litecoin achieves faster confirmation times, which represents a significant improvement in terms of processing efficiency.

But what has been said, although there are other currencies that solve Bitcoin's slowness, they have other problems inherent in its structure and all of them lack real adoption. And, in any case, I insist, it is not the objective of the book to discredit all alt-coins only Bitcoin specifically.

# YOUTUBE, TROLLS, AND OTHER NONSENSE

At the beginning of this book, I mentioned how a YouTube video about Bitcoin acted as one of the catalysts that motivated me to read this book. The responses I received in the video ranged from highly informed - albeit skewed by that dominant narrative - to those that defied all logic or were downright absurd.

What struck me deeply was not only the diversity of opinions, but the intensity with which certain positions were defended, even those that seemed to challenge the most basic principles of economics, technology, or even common sense. There were comments venturing into conspiracy theories to others presenting fundamental misinformation about Bitcoin itself that they defended.

Confronting such responses is a unique and futile challenge. On the one hand, I cannot help but try to correct, educate, or at least elevate the discussion and guide the conversation to a more nuanced and accurate dialog of Bitcoin and the underlying technology. On the other hand, some of the claims were so counterintuitive or so firmly rooted in misperceptions that finding a starting point for dialog was in itself impossible - much less trying to convince.

Although I am professionally dedicated to eCommerce and digital marketing, living firsthand this one further accentuated my view on the knowledge gap and the polarization around Bitcoin and the crypto world. The challenge, therefore, is not to counter disinformation, but to do so in a manner understandable to the general audience and respectful of those who, for several reasons, have reached hugely different conclusions and blind faith about BTC.

Leaving aside the insults and attacks on me, let us look at a couple of those surprising arguments in favor of BTC.

## IDEAL FOR EVADING TAXES, ILLEGAL MARKET, OR ILLEGAL SUBSTANCES

One comment that caught my attention is Bitcoin's defense of its use to not tax 'if you know how to do it.'

A comment that would also not be very worth answering because I do not think that, precisely the millions of users and crypto gurus, investment funds, etc. use it for that or think that precisely its value lies in its utility to evade taxes.

The irony is that cash has traditionally been considered the least traceable option by police and government entities and much less traceable than cryptocurrencies because of its physical and anonymous nature. When exchanging cash, there are no direct digital records of the transaction, making cash less transparent and more difficult to track.

In contrast, cryptocurrencies, such as Bitcoin or Ethereum, operate on blockchain technology. This is a distributed, decentralized database that records all transactions in cryptographically secured and linked blocks of data, making them immutable and, theoretically, "unhackable." The main advantage of blockchain is its transparency and traceability; each transaction is visible to all network users, ensuring constant verification and tracking.

Thus, although cryptocurrencies offer some degree of anonymity, as transactions are made through public addresses that are not necessarily linked to real-world identities, all transactions are fully traceable within the blockchain. This means that while you can transact anonymously, once an address is associated with a real identity, the full transaction history of that address becomes accessible.

This traceable character of cryptocurrencies represents a pole opposite to that of cash: while cash can be exchanged without leaving a direct record, cryptocurrencies leave a permanent digital trail on the blockchain.

So, while it's true that "if you know how to do it right" you can maintain a certain degree of privacy when using cryptocurrencies, it's also true that, by their nature, cryptocurrencies will always be tracked, offering a balance between anonymity and transparency that is not found in the use of traditional cash.

Evade taxes with BTC all you want, but if they detect you, they will literally expose all the fraudulent moves you have made.

## BIG FORTUNES AND BANKS BACKING BTC

Another published argument, passing a grammatical short correction filter, was to say that imagine the world's billionaires and largest investment funds risking their money in a "scam" with a digital asset like Bitcoin and it would not make sense that it did.

In case one needs to answer, billionaires and large investment funds do not "risk" in the conventional sense because, for them, money abounds, even when it comes to speculative high-risk investments. For these millionaires and funds, the relative share that they represent in their equity or investment portfolio is incredibly low; in contrast to what it would represent for those they try to convince.

In any case, none of them - neither millionaires, nor funds - makes them immune from bubbles, scams, and dubious financial products. They can just afford it; can you?

A more recent example, although smaller in scale and power, is the bubble of NFT (Non-Fungible Tokens). These digital assets theoretically offer tangible benefits, but their use has been mostly speculative to date. NFTs' promise to own sole ownership of unique digital assets attracted both serious investors and speculators. But misunderstanding and volatility have marked their trajectory in the market - a bubble and 100% speculative trajectory on which almost all the money invested has devalued.

A more appropriate comparison in terms of size could be the 2008 financial crisis, characterized by a real-estate and financial bubble. Here, the complexity and confusion came from financial products like subprime mortgages and unstructured debt. These instruments, which were difficult to understand even by professionals in the sector and designed on purpose, became the center of a crisis that affected the global economy, leading to the rescue of numerous funds and financial institutions. So, yes, funds and millionaires can also be cheated or fall into their own trap... but they were bailed out by governments - by printing money, something that just could not be done with BTC.

This episode illustrates how, in an intricate and globalized financial system, even the largest institutions can be engulfed in high-risk situations, not because of a lack of capital, but because of the complexity and lack of transparency of the financial instruments they handle. Thus, even if they have vast resources, the notion of "risk" is transformed, being more a matter of understanding and managing the complexity and implications of their investments than of the availability of capital per se.

I insist, for them it is a negligible portion and what they do is they buy their Bitcoin and then they buy real tangible assets (real estate) and other financial assets.

# A FINAL WORD

## 'FINFLUENCERS' AND TOXICITY

The book started with a disclaimer about my current position and my history of cryptocurrency investment. He said that transparency is the least that financial influencers could be asked to do ('finfluencers' if a term has to be put in). Behind these characters - yes, sometimes they are characters - there is a whole lifestyle folklore, of hidden interests behind the same cryptocurrencies or plain and simple what happens on all platforms: sensationalism to get more audience and monetize it through ads, undeclared sponsorships or as a door to other services - course on how to get rich in 3 weeks with crypto.

They usually inflate the results obtained, omit losses - all remarkably similar to the behavior of a Day trader or a compulsive gambler - or, at best, really are success stories... anecdotal. Not in the sense that its success - if it has, anyone can - cannot be replicated, but because the vast majority do not make money in the long run - or do not make it in the same dimension.

The problem is that everything that goes with Bitcoin - from sponsorships, celebrities, etc. - promotes a false sense of assured investment and there is nothing further from reality. Without going into the motives and the target audience of them, I consider that there is a greater toxicity behind cryptocurrencies than in other areas. Although there is now polarization and extreme discourse on virtually any issue, everything about cryptocurrencies unleashes passions - and hatred.

### THE HIDDEN FACE OF FINFLUENCERS

In recent years, the rise of cryptocurrencies has coincided with the emergence of numerous influencers in the investment arena, many of whom have focused specifically on the cryptocurrency market. This trend reflects growing interest in and fascination with the potential for quick gains. One concern, however, is that many of these influencers lack the knowledge and experience needed to provide sound financial advice - indeed, as a regulated sector, some make a disclaimer by washing their hands - posing risks to both themselves - legal and reputational - and their followers - of being scammed.

These influencers, with more charisma than experience, can quickly accumulate a wide audience on platforms such as YouTube, X, Instagram and TikTok. Their influence often extends beyond their actual knowledge, and the incentive behind it, in addition to the inherent pyramid scam, is the need to generate compelling content, extreme narratives, and, often, promises of easy money. But charisma and popularity are no substitute for financial education and investment experience, and the lack of these elements can lead to recommendations that are not well grounded in a solid understanding of the market or the very asset they seek to foster - in this case Bitcoin.

The problem is compounded when these influencers, motivated by personal gain, participate in promoting specific cryptocurrencies or investment products without adequate disclosure of the risks or their personal conflicts. In some cases, they have been involved in pump and dump schemes, where the recommendation of certain currencies is made with the aim of temporarily inflating their price and then selling at the peak, leaving their followers with a low value asset.

The ethical responsibility of providing investment advice is considerable, especially in a field as volatile and speculative as cryptocurrencies. The lack of regulation and the nature of social networks allow blurred lines between advice, manipulation or advice putting at risk the capital of inexperienced investors or those who trust the influencer of the turn.

For consumers of this content, it is crucial to develop critical thinking and due diligence before following influencers' cryptocurrency investment recommendations. This includes verifying your credentials, track record, and understanding that deep knowledge and experience cannot be replaced by enthusiasm or popularity on social media. The problem is that, for everyone to conduct their own research, when the dominant narrative is only on one side and, moreover, the user has certain biases... the result is obvious.

The lack of knowledge and experience of many influencers can trigger misunderstandings, bad decisions and, at worst, fraud, and manipulation, highlighting the importance of fostering financial education and accountability in both those who provide and those who consume financial information.

In addition, some influencers may participate in partnerships or receive sponsorships from cryptocurrency companies, exchanges or blockchain projects. In such cases, the economic incentive motivates them to take a biased or overly optimistic view of the products or services they promote - the classic: look the other way. While partnerships and sponsorships are common practices in many industries, in the realm of cryptocurrencies and influencers, where accurate and balanced information is crucial to making investment decisions, such bias can have significant consequences for small investors.

The lack of transparency about these interests and partnerships compounds the problem, as followers and the general public may not be aware of the actual extent and motivations of these recommendations. In the end, it is about investments based on charisma and popularity rather than grounded analysis.

Greater transparency and regulation in the disclosure of financial interests and conflicts of interest among influencers in the cryptocurrency space are essential to countering these problems. Fans and investors must also take a critical approach, questioning the motivation behind recommendations and evaluating information from multiple sources before making financial decisions.

It is crucial to foster a culture of honesty and accountability, where influencers adhere to ethical and disclosure standards, and where consumers of financial information are diligent and critical in their analysis - which already exist, but are not executed as they should.

In addition to the previously mentioned conflicts of interest, many influencers sell an attractive lifestyle to attract more followers and lack accountability for the statements and recommendations they make.

My criticism of the behavior of certain influencers in the cryptocurrency field does not imply a defense of the traditional practices of the banking and financial sector, which can also be questionable and sometimes misleading. It is just as blatant in one place as it is in another.

I recall one case where my bank's sales representative presented me with the results of a financial product that was divided into two parts. Part A showed an income of 50, while Part B recorded losses of -75. However, the consultant tried to make me believe that he had made money. I was literally trying to be stupid.

As I say, criticism of some - influencers - is not a defense of others - traditional advisers.

This type of practice, where numbers are "made up" or information is presented in a way that confuses or deceives the customer, is not unique to one sector or another; it is found both in the world of traditional finance and in the emerging cryptocurrency market. The impact of these tactics underlines the importance of transparency, honesty, and integrity in financial communication, as well as the need for consumers to be critical and well informed.

As with cryptocurrency influencers who manipulate information to attract followers or investors, financial advisers and other professionals may have incentives - ahem, commissions, ahem - to represent investment products in ways that hide their flaws or risks. This behavior is not only ethically questionable, but can also have detrimental financial consequences for customers making decisions based on this misinformation or incomplete information.

This personal anecdote only highlights the need for criticism, diligence and verification of the information received. Here and in the crypto world. Maintaining a critical approach, seeking the truth, and demanding transparency must be imperative for us.

And now, think of all those people who are in a more vulnerable situation and how difficult it can be for them.

## VULNERABLE TO TOXICITY

The phenomenon of polarization and edginess is not unique to any specific field, but it is undeniable that certain topics, such as cryptocurrencies, act as catalysts for these dynamics, attracting not only enthusiasts and skeptics, but also a darker spectrum: trolls and haters.

The culture and subcultures that form around cryptocurrencies are particularly susceptible to these phenomena because of the mix of anonymity, financial interests, and the sometimes fanatical passion of their communities. This environment can become a breeding ground for toxic behaviors, where harassment, insults, and attempts at emotional or financial destabilization become common tools for those seeking to provoke or harm others.

Anonymity and relative lack of consequence allow individuals to act with hostility that they might not express face to face. In the context of cryptocurrencies, where opinions can be extremely polarized and financial interests - money - are at stake, this dynamic intensifies. Trolls and hackers use any technique to destabilize a narrative that does not suit them, from disinformation, personal attacks to other methods of bullying to silence those with opposing views or simply to sow discord and chaos.

Moreover, the speculative and volatile nature of cryptocurrencies adds a layer of emotional strain to conversations. People's investments and savings are at stake, which can make discussions particularly heated and some individuals resort to destructive tactics in an attempt to influence the market or public perception. This not only affects the tone and quality of cryptocurrency discussions, but can also have real consequences on people's lives, from emotional stress to tangible financial impacts.

Recognizing and addressing toxicity in cryptocurrency communities is critical to ensuring that debate and discussion can continue in a productive and respectful manner. It is necessary to foster a culture of open and constructive dialog, where differences of opinion can be expressed without recourse to harassment or personal disqualification. This includes establishing clear rules and policies in forums and discussion platforms, as well as promoting education and critical thinking among participants.

The presence of trolls and haters in cryptocurrency conversations is, unfortunately, a reality that those interested in this field must deal with. But by addressing these toxic behaviors proactively and fostering a community based on mutual respect and the exchange of ideas, it is possible to create a healthier and more enriching environment for all. This not only improves the quality of discussions, but also contributes to a more nuanced and comprehensive understanding of cryptocurrencies and their potential impact on society.

My personal experience with harassment in the cryptocurrency arena, while mild, has been a telling window into the intensity and hostility that can arise in these conversations. Through comments and emails addressed not only to my arguments, but also to myself, I have felt the impact of an environment that sometimes prioritizes attack over constructive debate. This experience underscores the reality that participating in discussions on polarizing issues, such as cryptocurrencies, can expose a person to negative behaviors, where harassment and personal attacks are used as tactics to intimidate or silence.

These attacks not only sought to refute my views on Bitcoin and cryptocurrencies, but also attempted to discredit me personally and professionally. This strategy of attack seeks, in many cases, to undermine credibility and silence voices that present a critical or divergent view.

These incidents of harassment reveal how the discussion about cryptocurrencies can transcend the limits of a rational and technical debate to move into the personal and emotional realm. When confronted with these experiences, it becomes clear that there are individuals and groups who stop at nothing to defend their stance or interests in the cryptocurrency world, even if that means resorting to intimidation or slander tactics.

This type of behavior is not only harmful to the individuals who experience it, but also has a corrosive effect on the cryptocurrency ecosystem as a whole. It deters open and honest participation and creates an environment where people may feel reluctant to express contrary opinions or raise critical questions for fear of reprisals. Addressing these behaviors and establishing standards of conduct that promote respect and the exchange of ideas are crucial to fostering healthy debate and an inclusive community.

My personal experience in this area underscores the importance of creating safe and respectful spaces for cryptocurrency discussion, where ideas can be shared and debated without fear of personal attacks. It is essential that the cryptocurrency community work collectively to eradicate harassment and foster a constructive dialog that can enrich the understanding and adoption of these technologies. Ultimately, overcoming these challenges is critical to ensuring that the cryptocurrency space is accessible, equitable, and productive for all participants.

From my perspective, I have always tried to express my opinions and analysis on Bitcoin and cryptocurrencies from a place of respect, avoiding the use of insults or personal attacks. My intention has been to contribute to dialog and collective understanding with well-founded and reasoned arguments, even when I question or criticize aspects of these technologies. So it does not seem far-fetched to expect other people's interactions and responses to respect the same level of decorum and courtesy.

The call for respectful and constructive dialog should not be exceptional, but the norm in any debate, especially in fields as innovative and transformative as cryptocurrencies. Mutual respect in discussions not only reflects maturity and professionalism, but also fosters an environment where ideas can be productively and enrichingly exchanged and discussed.

Víctor de la Fuente

In an area as complex and nuanced as Bitcoin, where opinions are varied and interests are often conflicting, it is crucial that the dialog remains in a tone that favors understanding and collaboration. When conversations drift toward insult or contempt, the opportunity to learn from others' perspectives and advance collective understanding of these issues is lost.

Of course, not everyone will agree with every point or perspective that I present, and debate and disagreement are fundamental to the progress of knowledge and innovation.

However, disagreement does not need to translate into contempt or disrespect. An effective dialog on cryptocurrencies—or on any issue, really—should be able to be sustained on the merits of the arguments presented, not on the ability of one party to denigrate or discredit the other.

So, while some may consider naive the desire for respectful dialog in a field often marked by polarization and strong emotions, I argue that aspiring to an exchange of ideas in a tone of mutual respect is not only reasonable, but essential.

Therefore, criticize all you want the arguments - not the person - and in any case, do it with respect.

# CONCLUSIONS

At the beginning of the book I tried to make the structural problems of Bitcoin bluntly and clearly, and without the need for an additional 100 pages. Now to conclude, and I hope you do not feel deceived, I will condense the book into one sentence:

The long-term value of Bitcoin as a currency is €0 because its use as such is literally unfeasible; any other use is, if not questionable, purely speculative and its value is irrelevant (it can be worth €100,000 or €10) since its actual use is non-existent.

It is as simple as that, until now, the value of Bitcoin has fluctuated based on nothing tangible since, it is hardly used for what it aspires to be: a digital currency. At the same time, I am not saying that it has no value if it is used as a mere speculative instrument, but, then, let us not fool ourselves - or worse, deceive others - by linking BTC to hypothetical uses and scenarios of a future that difficult if impossible will happen or be realistic with the times.

I insist, I am not saying that you cannot make money investing in Bitcoin just like you can make money with roulette. But in both cases, we will not mask under an unreal narrative what is now, and will likely remain for a while, a purely speculative instrument.

# RESOURCES

"Digital Gold: Bitcoin and the Inside Story of the Misfits and Millionaires Trying to Reinvent Money" by Nathaniel Popper

"The Age of Cryptocurrency: How Bitcoin and Digital Money Are Challenging the Global Economic Order" by Paul Vigna y Michael J. Casey

"Attack of the 50 Foot Blockchain: Bitcoin, Blockchain, Ethereum & Smart Contracts" by David Gerard

"Bitcoin: Economics, Technology, and Governance" by Rainer Böhme, Nicolas Christin, Benjamin Edelman, y Tyler Moore. Published on "Journal of Economic Perspectives".

"The Bitcoin Boom: Asset, Currency, Commodity or Collectible?" by Aswath Damodaran

"Why Bitcoin is bullshit, explained by an expert" by Timothy B. Lee, interview with David Gerard. Published on Vox.

## ABOUT VICTOR DE LA FUENTE

Step into the world of Víctor de la Fuente, a visionary online marketing professional and adventurer born in Barcelona, whose life philosophy is as broad as his international career. His disruptive style brings a much-needed breath of fresh air to the various fields in which he operates.

In the professional sphere, Víctor is a driving force in the digital world. He has designed global e-commerce strategies for giants such as Nestlé, where he leads the worldwide e-commerce strategy, particularly in Retail Digital Media (e.g., Walmart, Carrefour, Amazon) and Social Commerce (e.g., TikTok, Instagram). His career spans from mid-sized companies to agile startups, always at the forefront of eCommerce and digital marketing. Beyond his core professional path, he not only works as a consultant through his own agency, vdelafuente marketing, but is also a seasoned entrepreneur: he co-founded a pioneering fashion app and explored other business models such as dropshipping. His digital expertise is deep and covers every area of marketing and e-commerce.

Beyond his professional focus on marketing, Víctor's true calling lies in education. He actively trains the next generation of professionals as a master's and postgraduate lecturer at several universities and business schools, specializing in eCommerce, social media, and entrepreneurship. His mission is not just to share knowledge, but to spark critical thinking, conveying firsthand the lessons learned in an industry that was still in its early stages when he began. It's also common to see Víctor de la Fuente at major eCommerce and digital marketing events, either as a keynote speaker or as part of roundtables.

What truly defines Víctor on a personal level, however, is his unbreakable spirit of adventure and transformation. He broke away from routine to embark on a 7-month solo backpacking journey around the world. This unique experience of exploration and growth, crossing countless countries, opened his mind to profound insights. Equally significant is his passion for sports, which has driven him not only to complete marathons but also to conquer mountain ultramarathons and similar challenges across different countries, showcasing his extreme endurance and personal resilience.

These intense professional and personal journeys have shaped in him a unique vision of life, inspired by timeless philosophies such as stoicism, Buddhism, and minimalism-essentialism. With a global and multicultural outlook, Víctor de la Fuente's central goal is to promote critical thinking applied to all aspects of life. His direct, no-nonsense, and often disruptive style seeks to provoke reflection, offering both high-level inspiration and practical day-to-day advice. Author of several books, including one on minimalism to which he feels particularly attached, Víctor embodies the very principles he defends.

Author, forward-thinking eCommerce expert, tireless runner, serial entrepreneur, and passionate educator, Víctor de la Fuente does not merely observe the future: he has lived it, shaped it, and now invites you to reflect critically on it. He challenges boundaries and builds a future with purpose.

# OTHER BOOKS BY THE AUTHOR

The inconvenient truth about Bitcoin. DE LA FUENTE, VICTOR. 2024

Stoicism and Zen Buddhism in Modern Life. DE LA FUENTE, VICTOR. 2023

Digital detox. DE LA FUENTE, VICTOR. 2023

The Win Strategy and other essays. DE LA FUENTE, VICTOR. 2023

Cyberbullying: IRL crisis. DE LA FUENTE, VICTOR. 2023

Learn ChatGPT. DE LA FUENTE, VICTOR. 2023

Against utopia. DE LA FUENTE, VICTOR. 2022

Smart Simple Investment Strategy. DE LA FUENTE, VICTOR. 2021

Poems from a metal heart. DE LA FUENTE, VICTOR. 2021

365 quotes and meditations. DE LA FUENTE, VICTOR. 2021

Minimalism: live better with les. DE LA FUENTE, VICTOR. 2016

www.ingramcontent.com/pod-product-compliance
Lightning Source LLC
Chambersburg PA
CBHW070154230526
45471CB00002B/659